PETER MAURIN

Prophet in the Twentieth Century

PETER MAURIN

Prophet in the Twentieth Century

BY

Marc H. Ellis

 PAULIST PRESS *New York/Ramsey*

ISBN: 0-8091-2361-4

Library of Congress
Catalog Card Number: 81-82338

Published by Paulist Press,
545 Island Road, Ramsey, N.J. 07446

Printed and bound in the United States of America.

Contents

TO
RICHARD L. RUBENSTEIN
WHO OPENED TO ME THE WORLD OF IDEAS
AND TO
WILLIAM D. MILLER
WHO GAVE ME A WAY OF LIFE

I can speak only of what I know. And what I know—which sometimes creates a deep longing in me—is that if Christians made up their minds to it, millions of voices—millions I say—throughout the world would be added to the appeal of a handful of isolated individuals who, without any sort of affiliation, today intercede almost everywhere and ceaselessly for children and for men.

Albert Camus—a statement
made at the Dominican Monastery
of Latour-Maubourg in 1948

*Peace be to thee. Our friends salute thee.
Greet the friends by name.*

3 John 14

PREFACE

In his book *The Diary of a Country Priest,* Georges Bernanos wrote: "How little we know what a human life really is—even our own. To judge us by what we call our actions is probably as futile as to judge us by our dreams." Though Bernanos was not referring to Peter Maurin, the mystery of human life evoked in the passage applies especially to Maurin's life. What do we really know of a man who, though his writings were circulated around the country and he spoke at length with hundreds of people, was a wanderer and revealed little of his background or interior life, even to his best friends? What words can convey the inner life of a man who decided in his fifties to give up everything he owned to embark on a life of voluntary poverty that the person and the social order might again be rooted in the teachings of Christ? How can one describe the mixture of tenacity, which saw him hold to this vision despite adversity, and gentleness, which proscribed harsh words or actions? Few modern biographers would subscribe to Bernanos's statement or to its corollary: that we can approach the meaning of a person's life only by preventing personal freedom from being objectified and defined. Thus, after studying Maurin for years and laboring at writing his biography, I can say without apology that Maurin's life remains a mystery.

For a variety of reasons this is not surprising. Maurin was in a certain way a prophet, and a prophet always remains a mystery. Coming from the past to critique and judge the present, the prophet proposes solutions that seem simplistic but that on closer examination are profound. He proposes ideas that challenge contemporary reality yet claims no originality. Though I have struggled to remain outside, inevitably I have been drawn into this mystery and have been changed by it.

Those who preceded me in writing about Peter Maurin have similarly been drawn into his mystery. The first and most prolific writer on Maurin was Dorothy Day, a woman who gained her vocation through his teachings. She invoked his presence in her columns in the *Catholic Worker* from its inception in 1933 and in her autobiographical books, *The Long Loneliness* (New York: Harper and Row, 1952) and *Loaves and Fishes* (New York: Harper and Row, 1963). It goes without saying that her recording of Maurin's thoughts and activities has been invaluable to my own work. Brendan Anthony O'Grady has also written about Maurin in "Peter Maurin, Propagandist" (Ph.D. diss., University of Ottawa, 1954), a work that explores Maurin's technique of agitation. Especially helpful to me were O'Grady's appendices, which contained letters from Maurin's family and friends and gave details and insight into Maurin's life prior to the founding of the Catholic Worker movement. Yet another writer, Arthur Sheehan, was a friend and disciple of Maurin's, and he attempted the first biography of Maurin, *Peter Maurin: Gay Believer* (New York: Hanover House, 1959). As a friend, Sheehan was privy to Maurin's activities and conversations, and as a biographer he was a diligent researcher, but proximity to his subject hindered objectivity to some degree, and his biography was also limited by the publisher's desire that personality rather than ideas be emphasized. Thus Maurin's most important years after the founding of the Catholic Worker movement are handled less than adequately. Though there has been another work since Sheehan's biography, one that attempted to trace the influence of Maurin's early life in France on his subsequent life and thought in America (Anthony W. Novitsky, "The Ideological Development of Peter Maurin's Green Revolution," [Ph.D. diss., University of New York at Buffalo, 1976]), Sheehan's research into Maurin's life in France remains the starting point for the reconstruction of the early part of Maurin's life. My debt to Sheehan is duly noted in Chapter 1.

PREFACE

William D. Miller is the most interesting of those who have written on Maurin for he was the first professionally trained intellectual to show interest in the Catholic Worker movement in general and Maurin in particular. In his book *A Harsh and Dreadful Love: Dorothy Day and the Catholic Worker Movement* (New York: Liveright, 1973), Miller posits Maurin as a gentle man who found his freedom in the Catholic tradition by voluntarily adopting poverty. The focus of Miller's work was on the story of the Catholic Worker movement, and at the same time he underscored the need for a full biography of Maurin. It is under his able (I would say inspired) direction that I have thought through Maurin's place in the twentieth century and completed the biography itself.

I am, however, grateful to Professor Miller for more than his insight into the life of Peter Maurin. Over the past five years at Florida State and Marquette universities, he has been generous with his time as a friend and as an intellectual. For me, as for others, he has shown the hospitality requisite to the development of a mature mind. Regardless of academic convention, and sometimes in the face of it, Professor Miller has encouraged me to pursue the meaningful questions of our time. It is not an exaggeration to say that he has given me a context for my own thought and writing, hence a vocation. To no person do I owe a greater debt than this.

Without exception my teachers have been a blessing. To my teachers at Florida State University in the religious studies department, Lawrence Cunningham, Richard L. Rubenstein, and Ann M. Vater, and to Paul J. Piccard in the political science department, I am grateful. Through their example of study and concern, they urged me to study and reflect. I owe special thanks to Professor Cunningham, who labored many hours on this manuscript. He has continually surprised me with his promptness and attention to detail, and with his encouragement to continue. It is a pleasure to work with him.

My teachers in the department of history at Marquette University are similarly deserving of thanks for their interest and diversity of gifts. Rev. Francis Paul Prucha, S.J., has been helpful in providing the scholarly technique that encourages mature reflection. Robert Hay, as chairperson of the department during my stay at Marquette, was instrumental in allowing me the freedom to construct my own program of study, as he was in helping me to secure consecutive Walter J. Schmitt Foundation fellowships. These fellowships provided me two years of financial support to pursue my studies and writing, and to Professor Hay and the Schmitt Foundation I am grateful. Michael Phayer has been a friend and with patience gave me a historical grounding in German history. I am grateful for both. I have also met and become close to three other professors at Marquette, without whom my education and life would have been lacking: Michael Fleet in political science, and James Robb and Mary Rousseau in philosophy. They have become models for me in their combination of intellectual and religious commitment. But the two without whom my sense of community at Marquette would have been hopelessly incomplete are Sebastian Moore and Matthew Lamb. Monks and intellectuals, they continued to convince me that the committed life, in spirit and intellect, has few rivals.

I am deeply indebted to the staff of the Marquette University Archives, especially the director, Charles Elston, and the curator of the Dorothy Day–Catholic Worker Collection, Phillip Runkel. Mr. Elston has been more than generous in the financial and moral support he lent my efforts, and Mr. Runkel has provided an expert knowledge of the collection as well as an unfailing desire to be of service. In the long hours in the archives they provided me with a sense of community. The support of the archives also allowed me to travel and interview those who had known Maurin well: Dorothy Gauchat, Marge Hughes, Stanley Vishnewski, Sister Peter Claver, and Elizabeth Sheehan. To these friends of Maurin's I am grateful.

Likewise I am indebted to the people who spent long hours working directly on the manuscript: Kathy Reck, typist; Mary Pittassi, proofreader; Joan Saleheh, who helped with translating. I am especially grateful to Ann McDonald, my wife, without whose patience and consistent editorial assistance this book would have been more difficult to write and less readable in its final form.

Finally, I would like to thank the Maryknoll School of

PREFACE

Theology and their Institute of Justice and Peace for inviting me to become a member of the faculty. In this connection I would like to thank Gene Toland and John Kaserow, members of the Maryknoll Society. I can think of no greater honor than to be among those who serve the poorest and the least.

INTRODUCTION

The Prophetic Voice in the Twentieth Century

The twentieth century has seen myriad and widespread transformation wrought by social and political revolution. The triumph of urban-industrial life over rural-agrarian societies and the victory of bureaucratic processes over personal, traditional folkways are but two instances of such changes. Initially, the urge to transform and overturn old ways promised an end to ignorance, increased benefits from medical developments, and the replacement of oppressive regimes by "enlightened" rule. To ease the burdens of poverty and oppression was to participate in the grand design of liberating humanity. For many persons this was a great calling and to this calling all sacrifice was due, even that of life itself.

This desire to usher in a new world was not unique, nor was the willingness to sacrifice in fulfillment of that desire. The Hebrew prophets had demanded both sacrifice and transformation and Jesus, within that tradition, had asked for more: One should work not only to transform, but to love even those who oppose that transformation. Over time both the Jewish and Christian traditions gave birth to other prophetic figures who asked nothing less than revolution. However, if the revolutions of the twentieth century are, as many scholars have claimed, indebted to this Judeo-Christian tradition with its emphasis on the poor and the oppressed, such has not been acknowledged by the leaders of modern upheavals. In fact, the revolutions of this century have often been viewed as a rebellion *against* the Judeo-Christian tradition and as an attempt to replace what revolutionaries perceived to be the reign of God with the reign of humanity. Many modern revolutionaries sought to replace once and for all the qualities of synagogue and church that they perceived as stifling the peoples' passion for justice: superstition and religious authority.

After eighty years of social and political revolution, however, victors and victims are difficult to distinguish, for revolutions in the name of humanity have ended in orgies of murder. In just eighty years the world has moved through the terrible terrain of holocaust in Stalinist Russia, Nazi Germany, and Southeast Asia. A century begun in hope and fueled by the ideals of progress and sacrifice today seems at the precipice of its own extinction. The century of revolutionary reform has, in the words of Gil Elliot, become "the century of the dead."

"The century of the dead" is a phrase in need of explanation and perhaps, more to the point, in need of illustration, for it graphically illumines the burden of revolutionary change in our century. To help visualize the carnage, Elliot pictures these dead not as isolated beings mistakenly erased from life, but as a nation and a people caught in the conflagrations of our time. As Elliot describes it, the nation of the dead has a population as cosmopolitan in its origins as the United States and is comprised of between 80 and 150 million people, depending on the casualty accounts accepted as authoratative. The real growth of this nation began in 1914 with the outbreak of World War I and reached 20 million by the early 1920s. Highlighted by the Stalinist terror, the nation of the dead grew steadily over the next twenty years and reached 40 million by the outbreak of World War II. During that war the population more than doubled, with annual increases peaking at ten to twelve million. Since 1945 the growth rate of the nation has declined but, as Elliot points out, this decline has been accompanied by a tremendous increase in the capacity for expansion. For Elliot, then, the nation of the dead is not past but future. If some postulate that the next century will be the century of Brazil or China, Elliot believes that it may well belong to the nation of the dead.[1]

INTRODUCTION

Like any nation, the nation of the dead has a landscape, and Elliot's description is worth quoting at length:

> The landscape might begin with that broad diffusion of death over the plains and poor hills of China and Mexico dislocated by war and revolution; with life draining back from exhausted towns into the countryside and into Novgorod. The peasants of these vast provinces ... wither under the blight of manmade famine, [as] marching armies uproot them from shallow misery and leave them on the bare earth battered and bleached like old cardboard boxes smelling sour in the sun and rain. You might see somePsuch landscapes as familiar, others with fresh surprises like waking on a long train journey as rings of dusk creep in the hills recalling new countries and old stories: and indeed the citizens of these parts are cosmopolitan and have many stories. Nigerians and Germans alike squeezed to death by economic blockade, Armenians massacred in the gaps between large and small wars, train-loads of Europeans dying between frontiers: Paraguayans, Chinese, French, Americans falling to disease in the intervals of fighting. Truly a universal nation, of which impressions must be as fleeting as those tantalizing glimpses of quiet static things from a train window, in the foreground rushing past and in the distance a slowly revolving panorama.... When it comes to an industrial landscape you cannot see so much, apart from general greyness, black chimneys, slag heaps and waste pools, from a train window. But of course! the railway sidings, so important to those nineteenth-century regions of the dead. The labour camp regions, with Vorkuta and Karaganda at the very end of those railway lines that push up into the Arctic and the east, down into Siberia and the south. The thick-clanging trucks that took the living and half-living from the ghetto regions of Poland, Russia and the Baltic States: and pumped eager uniformed lads into the battle regions of the Western front, the Ukrainian front, the Don, the Caucasus, the Italian front. The concentration camps with their own railway sidings.[2]

It is important here to pause and reflect on this landscape in theory as well, for reflection of this kind begins to alter our perception of the world we have inherited. Albert Camus is useful in creating such a perspective. Writing in the 1950s, Camus explored the infidelity of modern revolutions to their own promise: that is, while desiring to uproot oppression, revolutions instead continued that oppression under the banner of ideology. "In more ingenuous times," Camus wrote,

> when the tyrant razed cities for his own greater glory, when the slave chained to the conqueror's chariot was dragged through the rejoicing streets, the mind did not reel before such unabashed crimes, and judgment remained unclouded. But slave camps under the flag of freedom, massacres justified by philanthropy or by a taste for the superhuman, in one sense cripple judgment. On the day when crime dons the apparel of innocence—through a curious transposition peculiar to our times—it is innocence that is called upon to justify itself.[3]

According to Camus, the transposition of innocence to criminality is at the center of the twentieth century's infidelity to revolutionary reform, prompting the following conclusion:

> We are living in the era of premeditation and the perfect crime. Our criminals are no longer helpless children who could plead love as their excuse. On the contrary they are adults and they have a perfect alibi: philosophy, which can be used for any purpose—even for transforming murderers into judges.[4]

However, the juxtaposition of murderers with judges and the concomitant growth of the nation of the dead is not solely the province of revolution gone sour, though the growth of ideology seems intimately related to the failure of revolutionary reform. Both Elliot and Camus see this an international phenomenon in a world polarized by the militant ideologies of Marxism, fascism, and capitalism. In a world of militant ideology the person is submerged in conflicts that have less to do with ushering in justice than with the exercise of naked power.

The dangers of failed revolution and militant ideology do not stand alone, for they have taken on ominous qualities proportionate to the means at the disposal of the powerful. This has caused some to suggest that the major revolutions in the twentieth century have had less to do with the search for justice or changes in government than with the development of technology and forms of social organization that allow the assertion of totalitarian means to reach goals both good and evil. Unfortunately, the result is quite similar to that foreshadowed by Elliot and Camus: the relentless movement toward mass death.

That technology and social organization may account for the propensity *and* the ability of twentieth century political entities to create and enforce public policy in a totalitarian manner is the view developed by Richard L. Rubenstein in his recent book, *The Cunning of History: Mass Death and the American Future.* For Rubenstein, the holocaust of the Jews in Nazi Germany was a critical event in the twentieth century and in the history of Western civilization itself, but one that has essentially been misunderstood. The death camps were more than a testimony to Hitler's madness. They enlarged our conception of the state's capacity to do violence and, moreover, were an example of a systematic form of extermination made possible through the employment of technology and modern bureaucracy. In Rubenstein's view, the ramifications of this development are startling, with a previously unbreachable moral and political barrier now overcome. From that time on, systematic bureaucratically administered extermination of millions of citizens or subject peoples became one of the capacities and temptations of government. Though an event of this magnitude should call forth the energies of scholars and commentators, the burgeoning literature on the Holocaust still has not led to an understanding of the meaning of the event itself. Rubenstein sees this inability to comprehend the Holocaust as a failure to look at the event in the light of twentieth-century experience, that is, as a policy that could only have been carried out by a political community with a highly trained, tightly disciplined police and civil service bureaucracy achieved for the first time in the twentieth century.

The development of bureaucracy as an aspect of social organization was crucial to the implementation of mass death, and the policy that underlay these events designated peoples as superfluous to the functioning of modern society. In its organizational capacities the state now had the power to define who was within and who was outside the national community. As Rubenstein has noted, once defined as being outside the national community, and thus superfluous, these peoples were "condemned to segregated precincts of the living dead or exterminated outright." Like Elliot, Rubenstein sees the Holocaust not as past but as prologue, defining the Nazi experience as a warning for the future.[5]

All of this—the nation of the dead, the transformation of murderers into judges, and bureaucratically administered mass death—raises questions that in their magnitude are difficult to comprehend. Often as not, the complexity of the questions themselves is thought resolved in the assertion of inevitability. Here the massive change in ways and perception of life that has accompanied our century is summed up in the catchall phrase used by political scientists and historians—modernization. In short, the theory of modernization refers to the supplanting of traditional folk cultures, defined as religious, argrarian, and personal, with modern technological society, characteristically secular, urban, and bureaucratic. On another plane the shift can be seen as the movement of peoples oriented in local and religious traditions into a bourgeois world that, in splitting apart these traditions, seeks to redefine the development of individuality and the accumulation of material goods as the fruits of human existence. Involved are biases that define the process of modernization as both inevitable and progressive. However, to assert inevitability is to contravene the possibility of personal and societal choice, as it is to lose contact with the hopes and pain, the victors and vanquished, of a century of conflict. It is important to understand that the changes of our century for good and ill did not just appear; they became, and in their becoming were proposed by some and opposed by others. Progress, too, is suspect, for it is haunted by the cries of the dead and by those hundreds of millions who are separated from the structures that provide legitimation and affluence for an international elite but alienation and affliction for the majority of humankind. In many ways, those who have been left behind

INTRODUCTION

and injured in this process of modernization also comprise a nation and a people, which might be called the nation of the living dead. This has led John Murray Cuddihy to describe modernization as neither inevitable nor progressive but as a hurricane, destroying all in its path save those in the eye of the storm.[6]

If the intellectual constructs concerning inevitability and progress inform, indeed even dominate, contemporary education and culture *and* are suspect, we must begin the search for ways to better understand the world in which we live. The dichotomy between inevitability/progress and the grim realities we face often leads to confusion and paralysis. The literature of crisis, which has grown proportionate to the swelling legions of the dead, is itself an example of this confusion and paralysis—an acceptance of inevitable transformation but a protest against the results. Surely this literature has been important in showing that we share a common plight, yet to know only that we share a common plight in the present is to say that we are likely to share a common future as victims. While this demonstration of commonality is important, it requires clarification so as to raise the hard questions that lead beyond a solidarity of victims to a genuine movement of reclamation, a movement that broadens personal and societal options for the future. In other words, in the century of the dead it is not enough to be a victim. Those who survive must speak.[7]

Perhaps the paradox of our time is that, in an age that worships existential philosophy and culture, memory, and especially the memory of suffering, has a peculiar ability to clear away perceptions of life that have become trivialized and parochial. This insight has led the German theologian Johannes B. Metz to title a paper he delivered in October 1971 "The Future in the Memory of Suffering." In his paper Metz refers not to the memories that deprive the past of its substance and danger, as in the memory of "the good old days," but to the memory that makes demands of us:

> These are memories in which earlier experiences break through to the center-point of our lives and reveal new and dangerous insights in the present. They illuminate for a

13

few moments and with a harsh steady light the questionable nature of things we have apparently come to terms with, and show up the banality of our supposed realism. They break through the canon of all that is taken as self-evident, and unmask as deception the certainty of those "whose hour is always there." They seem to subvert our structures of plausibility. Such memories are like dangerous and incalculable visitants from the past. They are memories we have to take into account: memories, as it were, with future content.[8]

It is not an exaggeration to say that the remembrance of those who have died needlessly and violently is the beginning of fidelity to the breadth of human experience, especially as it presents itself to us now. Surely, though, if we are to be faithful to the memory of those dead and to the future, we must also remember those who have sacrificed on behalf of those who have suffered, and in so doing shared the suffering of others. To a large extent the recovery of their vision is participation in the recovery of a prophetic memory that has from the beginning of time subverted the commonly held understanding of the present. It should not surprise us that a century so dark has also given birth to men and women who have had prophetic thoughts and lived prophetic lives. And so in the century of the dead the question of the prophet is reborn.

The role of the prophet in the West has a long and arduous past, one that, like the nation of the dead, is more often forgotten than remembered. But the ancient Hebrew prophets and the tradition they embodied are worth recalling. These prophets rooted themselves in the past and present activities of God and were profoundly critical of contemporary values and social constructs that denied God's covenant with his people. It was the general treatment of the poor and the oppressed that provided insight into the neglect of the covenant. Thus the prophets spoke and indeed came for those who were suffering. Their message was reflected broadly throughout society, for the afflicted were signposts of the corruption of the affluent in the profanation of profit-centered business, the refusal to infuse values into commercial and social institutions, and resistance to serving the common good. However, it would be a mistake to see the prophets as social reformers. In the midst of judging human affairs, their task was to bring the world into divine focus and to unfold a divine plan. The rearrangement of social conditions was seen as a return to the correct ordering of the covenant and fidelity to God. Thus, in the act of proclaiming judgment the prophet made known the beginnings of a religious movement toward salvation.

In a profound sense, the meeting of the prophet and the community was an encounter that raised the deepest questions about social and religious existence. To a secular society the prophet brought the word of God; to a narcissistic community the prophet brought the message of service; to a people who proclaimed their own innocence the prophet was the harbinger of God's judgment. Confronting the present with the past, the modern with the ancient, coming from the hills and the desert, the prophet was like a deep and ancient memory encountering and unsettling the complacent and the unfaithful.

If the prophet *in his being* was a disturbing memory, he also provided a vision of the future: bleak if the community failed to return to God; hopeful if after hearing the Word the community returned. To a community intent on profits and pleasure, the prophet provided visions of the apocalypse and eschatology. The prophet, therefore, was never accepted as offering "practical" solutions to present ills but rather he challenged all that was practical and real.[9]

The prophetic tradition did not end with the Hebrew prophets. It was carried on and transformed by the greatest of all Jewish prophets, Jesus, and in the followers of Jesus through the development of the Christian tradition of sainthood. Similarities between the two traditions are many, with their emphasis on the sacred word, concern for the poor and the oppressed, and public proclamation that social arrangements and fidelity to God are one. There are differences as well, and it is fair to say that the saintly tradition has tended to diverge from the prophetic tradition in emphasis. While the prophetic tradition formed around judgment, immediacy, and the Word, the saintly tradition has tended to stress interiority, witness, and perseverance over time.

PETER MAURIN

One may legitimately ask what all of this has to do with life in the twentieth century. To the modern sensibility, the journey from the death camps in Nazi Germany to the Hebrew prophets and the Christian saints seems almost contrived, a whimsical construct in the face of unparalleled crisis. But to Simone Weil, a twentieth-century French activist and mystic, the continuing development of the prophetic and saintly tradition was not odd but urgent. In the midst of World War II and shortly before her own death Weil wrote:

> We are living in times that have no precedent, and in our present situation universality, which could formerly be implicit, has to be fully explicit. It has to permeate our language and the whole of our way of life. Today it is not nearly enough merely to be a saint, but we must have the saintliness demanded by the present moment, a new saintliness, itself without precedent.

To Weil, a new type of sanctity was as the newness of spring or the novelty of invention. If all was kept in proportion and the order of things preserved, a new revelation of the universe and of human destiny would emerge:

> It is the exposure of a large portion of truth and beauty hitherto concealed under a thick layer of dust. . . . Such a petition is legitimate, today at any rate, because it is necessary. I think that under this or any equivalent form it is the first thing we have to ask for now; we have to ask for it daily, hourly, as a famished child constantly asks for bread.[10]

The twentieth century has seen the creation of that which Weil thought essential: a new saintliness. Though not yet fully articulated, the essential outlines of such a saintliness can be postulated from the prophetic voices identifiable in our time. In broad terms, this seems to include a willingness to address directly and openly the questions of the day, to refuse the political and economic alternatives presented as "realistic," to attempt to recover the personal aspects of social and private life, to serve as a witness to or advocate for the poor and oppressed, and, finally, to move beyond the political into a religious vision. We might say that this new saintliness represents the co-alescence as well as the transformation of the traditions of prophet and saint in that judgment and interiority, immediacy and witness, the Word and perseverance are combined. Not surprisingly, this development has brought people from diverse backgrounds and traditions into a community of thought and action, but a community on the periphery of socio-political and modern religious consciousness. It may even be said that this community, insofar as it chooses to be with those "outside," the deprived and outcast, is itself outside, a community in exile. Among others, this community in exile is comprised of people such as Walter Benjamin, Martin Buber, Albert Camus, Dorothy Day, Mahatma Gandhi, and Simone Weil.[11]

Less well known but equally interesting in this context is Peter Maurin (1877–1949), a French peasant who emigrated to Canada, then to the United States, and founded the Catholic Worker movement in 1933 with Dorothy Day. In many ways Maurin contravened a way of life that was increasingly vaunted as the epitome of accomplishment. Instead of seeking security, Maurin was a wanderer, not only between countries but within the United States and even after he had ostensibly settled in New York State at the age of forty-eight. In a culture that stressed the freedoms of youth and affluence, Maurin was again atypical. His vocation as an agitator crystallized when he was in his fifties and to fulfill his vocation he embraced, as a layman, celibacy and poverty. To a presentist culture Maurin brought a vision from the past as he sought to move from the impersonalism of an urban-industrial society to the personalism of a rural-agrarian society. To a society characterized by institutional charity and secularity, Maurin endeavored to provide personal hospitality to the afflicted and to restore the communal aspects of Christianity as a way of restoring the spiritual dimensions of existence to culture and to the ordering of social life.

Despite the odds against the successful implementation of his vision, Maurin rarely felt alone in his concerns. As far as Maurin was concerned, he was fulfilling the Roman Catholic tradition he had inherited and participating, as others before him, in revealing that tradition's dynamism. To expose the

17

maladies of the present, Maurin drew heavily on this tradition, placing special emphasis on the prophets, the early Christians, the Church Fathers, the saints (especially Francis of Assisi) and the teaching authority of the popes.

But Maurin's sense of tradition was expansive and rarely ended in the past. Thus he sought out those who, in thought and activity, could help to clarify the position of contemporary believers. Many of Maurin's ideas were clarified by the thinkers and writers of his time. Accordingly, it would be fair to say that instead of being an originator, Maurin was a synthesizer who had the ability not only to communicate intellectual concepts to the person on the street but to embody these ideas as well. In these ways Maurin, in his person, brought to the masses the Catholic tradition and the thought of contemporary dissenting intellectuals.

The intellectuals that Maurin read came from a variety of schools of thought: the English Distributists who rejected machine technology and urban civilization for an agrarian, handicraft society; a revived Thomistic school of philosophy that sought to reassert the efficacy of metaphysics; the French Personalist school, which attempted to reestablish the centrality of personhood in the individual and the social realms. Many of the intellectuals Maurin read and quoted were well known and included G. K. Chesterton, Christopher Dawson, Eric Gill, Jacques Maritain, and Emmanuel Mounier. Others, like Nicholas Berdyaev and Vincent McNabb, were less well known. Though the threads that ran through these writings were diverse, the basic conviction emerged that the revival of the spiritual dimension in the person and the culture could reverse the decline of civilization initiated with the triumph of secularism in the eighteenth century. For most, the dignity of the person could be affirmed only when this dimension was recognized. A humanism without God was to set forces into motion that would take humankind into a new dark age, where all would be possible and permissible and the person would count for nothing. Accordingly, these thinkers feared the power of modern life seen in industrialism, urbanism, and statism. Because of these fears, Edward Shapiro has labeled this group "decentralist intellectuals," and others, with less insight, have termed them reactionaries. Neither label, however, does justice to the motivation of their thought or their intellectual capabilities. Instead, these intellectuals might be better understood as dissenters against the confusion and violence of a world emerging into modernity. In the light of our century's subsequent experience they should be seen as protesting against a slaughter that was just beginning.[12]

Like the tradition he affirmed and the intellectuals he read, Maurin, too, was a dissenter against modernity. His vision of community was neither evolutionary nor progressive and the appetite of modernity, in its search after power, held no lure for him. Instead, Maurin's vision was much simpler: to live in harmony with others, to share with the community what manual and intellectual labor had produced, to be silent and to worship in common. At the same time, Maurin's sense of commitment was also a dissent. He did not share the basis or the hopes of secular radicals and liberals for the reform of the social order, for they were seeking to increase and distribute the material abundance of industrial life to a humanity freed from the spiritual. Of this Maurin wanted no part. Instead of affluence, the basis of Maurin's commitment was renunciation and sacrifice as exemplified in the life and crucifixion of Jesus. It was in this life of spirit and sacrifice that Maurin grounded his ideas and saw the possibility of recapturing the integrity of the person and effecting social reform.

However, to see Maurin simply as a dissenter against modernity is to miss the foundation of his mission and life. To enter into the life and death of Jesus was to affirm a spiritual reality and to become a disciple and Maurin was, more than anything else, a disciple of Christ. This discipleship was not a peripheral attachment to an otherwise developed program of social reform, but was the center of Maurin's life from which his social apostolate came. It formed the basis of Maurin's oft-repeated statement that his word was tradition not revolution, though, he would hasten to add, a tradition made dynamic and faithful to its calling to represent Christ in the world.

Fidelity to Christ in the spirit was to mean fidelity to the body of Christ in the world, and in a world filled with injustice and death this was not easy. Among other things, participation in the body of Christ would demand love of neighbor out of which radiated the presence of God, and judgment could not occur solely on the external manifestations of a person's existence, economic class, or political persuasion. To recognize the worth of the person in relation to God was to enter a dilemma: the changing of a social order that hindered the spiritual development of the person became a necessity, at the same time making violence unacceptable even in the movement toward reform. Incarnation meant reform *and* nonviolence.

Maurin was not alone in living this dilemma of social change and nonviolence, for such notable figures as Martin Buber and Mahatma Gandhi also explored these questions and possibilities within their own traditions of Judaism and Hinduism. Though arrived at independently, their conclusions were startlingly similar. The world was moving, even hurtling, into darkness and only by charting a radically new direction would the person and the world survive. Paradoxically, this direction could come only through a revival of the traditions the modern world labored to forget, traditions that gave the person the proper due by placing him within the context of eternity. Buber looked at the synagogue and Gandhi at the ashram in the same way that Maurin looked at the Church: as a place of faith where the seeds of personal and societal conversion would be nurtured.[13]

Against the backdrop of the century of the dead the questions of tradition and the prophetic voices that came within it would be neither loud nor immediately successful. Indeed, among the affluent and powerful many of those voices would be dismissed and lost. However, for those who suffered, and for those who sought an end to their suffering, the witness and the voice would remain.

CHAPTER ONE

France
1877–1909

Aristide Pierre (Peter) Maurin was born on May 9, 1877, in the small French village of Oultet, the first child of Jean Baptiste Maurin and his wife Marie Pages. Peter's childhood was filled with the noise of children born and raised, prayers said, and some feeling for the beauty as well as the precarious quality of life on the land.[1]

Located in the commune St. Julien de Tournel in the Languedoc region of southern France, the Oultet area was noted for its mountains, isolation, and poverty. In the years of Peter's youth the village counted fifteen peasant families, most of whom spoke a dialect and who lived primarily by farming and tending sheep. The Maurin farm was situated on the left bank of the Lot River on the north slope of Mount Lozere, a mountain that served as a dividing line between Catholics who inhabited the northern slope and Protestants who gathered on the southern slope.

The Maurin farm was comprised of pastures and fields interspersed with uncultivated land and forests. Because of poor terrain the farm yielded little and the income from renting fields was negligible. The buildings located on the farm were simple. The house contained five rooms, with sheep kept in the basement, while two other buildings housed firewood and tools. The family produced basic peasant foodstuffs, with breads, cheeses, and vegetables providing the bulk of the Maurin diet.[2]

Peter was the first child of what was to become a large

family. Eighteen months after his birth a brother, Celestin, was born, followed two years later by a sister, Marie. Peter's mother was to bear two other children, who did not survive, and she herself died in childbirth in 1884. Little is known about her life except that she had a pleasant disposition and was known throughout the village as a charitable woman. Though the Maurin means were small, she rarely turned away travelers or the poor in need of help. In 1887, three years after the death of his first wife, Jean Baptiste married Rosalie Bousquet, who, at nineteen years of age, was much younger than he. She mothered the three Maurin children and bore nineteen more, making Peter the oldest of twenty-two children.

Jean Baptiste carried the mark of discipline and religiosity that had characterized his own father, Aristide Maurin. Aristide served as a model of faith to the Maurin family, reciting the Rosary and reading from the Bible daily. Jean Baptiste was also highly religious and possessed a deep knowledge of his faith, which he taught to his children. At home, evening prayer was conducted in front of a small statue of the Virgin Mary. For Sunday Mass the family walked to the parish church in the village of St. Julien de Tournel two miles away, and Peter journeyed there again on weekday mornings to attend catechism while preparing for his first holy communion. When winter made the roads impassable, Jean Baptiste led his family in prayers at home and sometimes recited them himself from memory. During meditation he would often speak to his children about the foolishness of those who thought only of the earthly life without concerning themselves with the spiritual.[3]

Peter began his formal education in Oultet in a little school with wood-shuttered windows and a stone doorstep. He received his *certificate d'études* at the age of fourteen and continued his studies at the *pensionnat* of St. Privat in Mende, twelve miles from Oultet, which was run by the Christian (De la Salle) Brothers. The curriculum of the school was innovative for its time and included secular subjects as well as catechetics, scripture, church history, and liturgy. As in all Christian Brothers' schools, the *pensionnat* had a spartan simplicity and a rich religious life. Great emphasis was placed on silence and prayer. Days began with the Angelus and Mass and ended with evening prayers; the sign of the cross and a short prayer opened each class. Morning devotions in Latin and afternoon devotions in French completed the cycle of prayer at the school.[4]

The Brothers at St. Privat would single out those youths whom they considered to have a religious vocation, and Maurin was one of those selected. On completion of his basic studies, he embarked on a two-year course of study at various institutions with the goal of entering the Christian Brothers' order. After spending a year at the junior novitiate at Buzenval in Sien et Oise, Maurin left for Paris late in the summer of 1893 to enter the *grand novitat* located at 27 Rue Oudinot near the Eiffel Tower. Here the life of the novice was bound up in spiritual formation, and in October of that year Maurin wore the habit of the Brothers for the first time. After the novitiate Maurin entered the scholasticate at St. Joseph's in Paris, where teaching methods and the psychology of education were emphasized. Here the Brothers prepared for their degrees and studied the life of De la Salle and the teaching methods set forth in his manual *The Conduct of Schools (La Conduite des Ecoles).*[5]

De la Salle's manual contained a theory of education as well as a detailed guide to the implementation of that theory. De la Salle emphasized the use of the native tongue in learning where only Latin was used before, and grouping children according to their knowledge and ability instead of massing them together regardless of differences. But for Maurin, the most important of De la Salle's theories was his view of the teacher as a model of sacrifice and devotion with the corollary that religious life and service to the poor would embody these principles. Clearly, this theory of sacrifice and devotion, with its implementation through working with the disadvantaged, appealed to Maurin, for it represented another dimension of his religious upbringing. These ideas were to have a lasting effect on him and provide the foundation for a life of teaching outside of the Brothers and the classroom, though this crystallized only in later years.

Maurin was drawn to this life of sacrifice and took his first annual vow in September 1895, taking the name of Brother Adorator Charles. For the next seven years, Maurin traveled from school to school in pursuit of his own vocation, while continuing in the teaching tradition of the Christian Brothers. His first assignment as a teacher was at the *grand pensionnat* at Passy, a middle-class suburb of Paris. During this time his brother Celestin also joined the Brothers. Their proximity allowed them to meet often and to discuss their views on the religious life and the world in general. Maurin was next transferred to Issy, another suburb of Paris, in February 1896 and was given a regular class at the Ecole St. Nicholas. Ten months later he was teaching fourth grade at the Charonne school located in a working class district.[6]

Although a member of a religious order, Maurin was still subject to military service and from November 1898 to September 1899 his religious vocation was interrupted by a call to serve as a soldier in the 142nd Infantry Regiment of Mende at Lodeve. This was a disturbing, perhaps even transformative, experience for him, for his superiors and his brother Celestin confirmed that he strongly objected to military service. The organization of people toward a dubious end undoubtedly disturbed him. His background as a peasant, with its lack of emphasis on nationhood, and as a Brother, with its emphasis on the poor, clashed with the assertion of national aspirations and protection of wealth bound up with the military. When his tour of service ended, Maurin received an honorable discharge and was placed in the reserve, which allowed the army to call him up periodically for training periods lasting several weeks. The disturbing issue of militarism thus remained. When he returned to his teaching post with the Brothers, Maurin began to read and reflect about the nature of social organization because of its coercive and destructive potential. In particular, he explored the possibilities of pacifism. His thinking on these questions was of such an intensity that it caused concern among some of his peers, who feared that his interest in social questions would disturb his religious vocation. The sole advantage of army life was that it brought him close to home, so he occasionally visited his family.

After three successive annual vows, Maurin professed his first three-year vows in 1899. That September he was sent to Neuilly, an affluent suburb of Paris, to teach the sixth grade. Transferring from a working-class district to an affluent suburb increased the availability of books and provided Maurin with an opportunity to continue his reading on politics and, at the same time, to become acquainted with current trends in literature and history. It was here that he further broadened his intellectual life by joining a lay study club that sought, under the guidance of priests, to study the social and religious questions of the day. This involvement with the study club signaled the beginning of Maurin's contact with a variety of Catholic social and religious perspectives, and the first intimations of his own understanding of a Catholicism that spoke beyond the farm and the classroom to the reshaping of the modern world.[7]

In the fall of 1900 Maurin was transferred to Versailles St. Louis. Here he taught the third grade until the following January when he was transferred to the Ecole Fenelan at Vaujours, eight miles from Paris. The estate, located on the land of the Joseph de Maistre family, was large and provided room for cultivation so that in addition to regular academic subjects students were taught gardening and horticulture. His own childhood on the land left Maurin adept at teaching farming to the orphans and abandoned children who were his students. His two year stay here was his longest as a teacher in one school.[8]

The continuing secularization of French life, begun in the tumult of the French Revolution, carried a legacy of discrimination and politicization for Catholics. With the elevation of Emile Combes to the position of premier in the election of 1902, politics intruded more directly on the Brothers and on Maurin himself. Combes, an ex-seminarian, was in the vanguard of those who sought to subordinate the Church to the state. A prime target for such a secular philosophy was education, and Combes began his term of office by closing religious schools throughout France. Eventually over 150,000 children were affected by the closings and though the pace slowed, primarily because of the vast educational disruption, the future of Catholic education in France seemed dim. Catholics realized that the issue of religious or secular education held wider implications than the schooling of the young, and Catholics all over France responded to this assault. Protests were initiated and associations formed. One of these associations, called *Le Sil-*

lon (The Furrow), held its first public meeting in 1901. In contrast to other associations, some of which favored the reinstitution of monarchy and the power of Church hierarchy, *Sillon* declared itself firmly in favor of the Republic, a republic infused with Christianity. It was *Sillon*'s belief that the French people would no longer tolerate irreligious republicans. Thus the role of *Sillon* was to prepare France for her future as a Christian republic.[9]

Maurin, aware of this volatile controversy, became increasingly attracted to the ideas of *Sillon*. His own vocation remained uncertain and his life as a religious was questioned by his superiors, who viewed Maurin's constant moving about with some trepidation. Indeed, Maurin's restlessness had increased rather than diminished in his years as a Brother, and his future, though to be intimately involved with teaching, lay beyond the formalities of the classroom. Later in life, Maurin explained his attraction to *Sillon* briefly, stating that the movement reflected the chaos of the times. In December 1902, after nine years with the Brothers and free of all obligations to them, Maurin, at twenty-five years of age, left to work with *Sillon*.[10]

Sillon, with which Maurin was associated for the next six years, was itself heir to a tradition of Catholic activism, a tradition awakened by the urban-industrial revolution and the forces of secularization that had attended it. A sense of urgency had been added by Leo XIII's encyclical *The Condition of the Working Classes (Rerum Novarum, 1891)*, which rallied the Church to the defense of the worker and raised in a dramatic way the role of the Church in the modern world. But though the tradition was complex and held within it notable and diverse figures, the two who would influence Maurin directly were Leon Harmel and Marc Sangnier.[11]

Leon Harmel was a democrat and his ideas were evidenced at Val-des-Bois in Champagne in his family's spinning plant, a model of industrial cooperation and religious revival. The program attempted to address what Harmel saw as the primary evil of industrialism, the creation and exploitation of an irreligious proletariat. Harmel's program included educational insurance and a factory council that encouraged worker participation in the technical and disciplinary control of the factory. Employee-employer associations were formed, and management recognized the obligation to provide a just wage and healthy conditions for the workers. In Harmel's view, responsibility went beyond maintenance of good physical conditions to the needs of the souls of the workers. Essential to the needs of the soul was a highly religious atmosphere and in actuality this existed side by side with industrial cooperation at Val-des-Bois. Close to the plant was a chapel where daily Mass was said and holidays observed; from this chapel grew charitable organizations that provided services to the sick and the needy of the area. Eventually both workers and management joined the Third Order of Saint Francis, a lay order dedicated to carrying out the piety and service of its founder, Francis of Assisi. To Maurin, Val-des-Bois represented an industrial concern that, by bringing management and workers together, furthered the bonds of community and encouraged the proper use of production for service to the community rather than for profit. Maurin was deeply impressed by the role that the Third Order of Saint Francis played in helping organize and solidify the virtues of charity practiced by the management and workers of Val-des-Bois. Clearly, Maurin read much about Harmel and was excited by the prospects of combining small and responsible industry with community and religious life. He may even have visited the plant in 1908 when he was traveling through the south of France. To those who in later years would accuse him of a bias against industry, Maurin would cite with approval Harmel's understanding of authority and the dignity of work.[12]

Such ideas provided the context for the new Catholic activism of *Sillon*, and Maurin plunged fervently into the movement in 1903. Here he came into contact with the final major figure of Catholic social action at the turn of the century, the founder of *Sillon*, Marc Sangnier.

The *Sillon* of Marc Sangnier favored the acceptance of a democratic order and, in the process, the Christianizing of it. For Sangnier, democracy represented the social order that nurtured a degree of conscience and responsibility in the person that was difficult to develop in autocratic societies. To establish a Christian democracy, an elite of young Catholics was necessary to enlighten the masses, and this enlightenment was to be accomplished through popular institutes and public meetings. In programmatic terms, *Sillon* favored the elimination of economic and political institutions that barred the way of workers achieving their rightful dignity; toward this end the establishment of consumer and producer cooperatives was sought. Hospices were established and pacifism preached. Above all, there was a mystical element to *Sillon*. The first mission of its members was to be penetrated with the thought of Christ and to make the presence of Christ dwell within the person and the social order.

Maurin actively participated in the activities of *Sillon*. Often he could be found distributing the movement's newspaper *Democratic Awakening (L'Eveil Democratique)* on the streets of Montparnasse and the Latin Quarter, as well as participating in the devotional life, which included all-night vigils. As participation in the movement was voluntary and unremunerated, Maurin sold coffee and cocoa to support himself, and took a cheap room in the Temple district of Paris at Rue de Santarges.[13]

Sillon's phenomenal growth was due mostly to Sangnier's charisma and the youth of his followers. With its growth, though, came a change in the movement's direction. By 1905, just two years after Maurin had entered the movement, *Sillon* was moving from a confessional organization to a political one, a direction Maurin would ultimately oppose. In 1907 Sangnier committed his energy to this new direction, announcing "the greatest *Sillon*" and calling for a new center of moral unity. This unity would include those who consciously or unconsciously animated the Christian spirit, leaving the door open for Protestants and other non-Catholics to participate. The shift in focus was most perceptible in *Sillon*'s understanding of mission: In 1903 *Sillon* understood its mission to live Catholicism, but by 1907 *Sillon* understood itself to be a lay movement working for the establishment of a democratic republic. *Sillon*'s final step toward politicization occurred in 1909–1910, when Sangnier sought political office and *Sillon* was divided into confessional and nonconfessional spheres. This shift in perspective occasioned a letter of condemnation in the summer of 1910 from Pius X, who thought that *Sillon* had lost its religious character and should disassociate itself from Catholic affiliation.[14]

In the early months of 1908, two years before the papal condemnation, Maurin left the movement. It was not by chance that his departure coincided with the organization and politicization of the movement. If Maurin had devoted his energies to *Sillon* because it had understood the chaos of the times, he left because it began to interpret the social question solely in political terms and had abdicated its original emphasis on the spiritual. Using a paraphrase of Abbé LeClerq, editor of *La Cité Chrétienne*, Maurin would later say of the movement:

> *Sillon* was full of enthusiasm and generosity but lacked deep thought. It allowed itself to present democracy as the only political regime in conformity with Christianity. It was condemned for the preceding reason as well as imprudence in thought and language.[15]

There was also the reason of temperament. Maurin, a considerate and gentle person, reacted negatively to demonstrations that were a part of *Sillon*'s activities and that inevitably encouraged violent clashes with toughs from other political and religious factions.

This distaste for violence existed outside the sphere of *Sillon* as well. In 1904 (August 22–September 8) and again in 1907 (December 2–22) Maurin had served time in the army reserve as part of his continuing military obligation after his discharge from the army. The prospect of once again rendering military service weighed heavily on him and forced a decision. After his second stint in the reserves Maurin no longer answered military summonses and changed his residence frequently to avoid the police.[16]

Maurin's continuing, albeit unwilling, involvement with the military and his departure from *Sillon* came during a time when advertising in France for Canadian settlers was increasing. Canada had distinct advantages for someone in his position. The French population of Canada was growing, and with that, the presence of French priests was assured; inexpensive farm land was available and there was no conscription. The thought of emigrating, though, was not easy, for by the age of thirty-one most of his contemporaries had their own families and had settled into their life's work. Maurin's leaving *Sillon* and contemplation of Canada signaled his failure as yet to find his own vocation. Maurin's background, too, provided little in the way of support for emigration, especially since the land the family inhabited had been passed down generation after generation for a thousand years. Surely the loss of contact with his family and the land would be difficult.[17]

But there was more involved here than the difficulties of emigration. Maurin had seen the Church and the world from a variety of perspectives—as peasant, teacher, and urban activist—and, while all contributed to his future, in the end they left him wanting. His desire to find his place within a tradition now reaching back two millennia, continued. When Maurin, in consultation with his family, decided to emigrate to Canada, it was done with the thought of leaving all behind and beginning anew, a beginning that was not to be easy.

CHAPTER TWO

Wanderings 1909–1933

Uncertain of his future, Maurin departed from Cherbourg on the American ship *St. Louis* in the summer of 1909 and landed in New York City several weeks later. He was fortunate to meet a Frenchman on board whose brother resided in Canada north of Prince Albert and, having become friends, Maurin accepted the man's invitation to his brother's home. The brother was well-to-do and generous, and he loaned Maurin a sum of money to begin his new life. Setting out on his own, Maurin met another man who later became his partner in a joint homesteading venture in Saskatchewan. Neither the location of their homestead nor the name of his partner is known. However, it is known that communication between the two was difficult, for at this time Maurin spoke no English and his partner spoke no French. The language barrier was compounded by the difficulties of settling virgin land, for the severity of winter and lack of funds made the life of the homesteader difficult.[1]

The following year Maurin's partner was killed during a hunting expedition and, unable to work the homestead alone, Maurin left to work in the wheatfields in Alberta province. Soon after, he dug ditches in irrigation projects for the Canadian Pacific Railway, and traveling east to Ottawa he quarried stone. He tried lumberjacking in the Adirondacks as well but found the climate too damp.[2]

In 1911, penniless and still speaking only French, Maurin decided to come to the United States. The years to follow would allow little stability in his life as he wandered from job to job throughout the breadth of the country. His first stop was Ogdensburg in northern New York State, where he secured a temporary job tearing down concrete forms. Low on funds, Maurin left for New York City, and leaving there almost immediately begged his way through Baltimore, Washington, Cumberland, and across the Maryland border into Pennsylvania. Here he was arrested for vagrancy, a story often recounted by Maurin. One day in his travels Maurin had wanted a drink of water and proceeded to knock on the door of a nearby house. A woman appeared and tried to open the door, but it had become stuck by frost. Maurin started pushing to help her open the door. The neighbors, thinking he was trying to break in, called the sheriff. Although uncertain if any wrong had been committed, the police put him in jail to please the neighbors. In the following days, however, the townspeople became acquainted with Maurin and finally sought his release. The sheriff, once again to please the neighbors, set Maurin free.

In the winter of 1912 Maurin traveled to the coal regions of western Pennsylvania and took a mining job with the Henry Clay Frick Coal and Coke Company at one dollar and fifty cents a day. He lived in one of the unused coke ovens with a black co-worker, the two keeping warm in the heat from an oven operating next door to them. Maurin later recalled that it was a simple life, for "all you had to do was to crawl in and lie down and you were at home." A brush with danger was the only other incident of note. Maurin related that he was digging a ditch to keep the hillside from sliding when a boulder broke loose and thundered past within arm's reach.

In 1913 Maurin left Pennsylvania and rode the rails to Akron, Ohio, where he worked for two dollars a day with a building contractor. From there he moved to a paint shop in Chicago. Once again working for the railroad, Maurin was sent to work at the Galena lead mines near Dubuque, Iowa, piling rocks for seventeen and a half cents an hour. When the boss tried to cut wages to seventeen cents an hour, Maurin quit. However, he had to go to Chicago to get his final paycheck from the railroad, riding, as he put it, "IOU." In Chicago he was again arrested, this time for riding the railroad without paying, and he spent several days in jail.

WANDERINGS

From the time of his release from the Chicago jail until America's entry into World War I in 1917, Maurin continued his travels through the Midwest, laboring at jobs similar to those he had held before with railroads, in sawmills and doing janitorial work. His longest tenure of employment was two years with a dry goods store on Chicago's South Side. When he thought he ought to have a raise and the owners did not offer one he quit rather than ask.[3]

With America's entry into the war, the need for French teachers as translators and army officers became acute. Maurin offered lessons in French and eventually developed a small school in which he employed several teachers. Located in Chicago, the school was successful enough to last eight years and make Maurin a fairly affluent man. Maurin had not corresponded with his family for years, primarily it seems because of his status regarding military service in France, but now, somewhat settled in America, he wrote home again. In the resumption of the correspondence Maurin learned of his father's death near the end of the war. One of his brothers had been lost in the war and one of his sisters had become a nun and was directing a school in Bolivia. He also found that Celestin, his younger brother, had been teaching as a Christian Brother in Pueblo, New Mexico. However, neither knew of their proximity, and Celestin had finally returned to France when the war began.[4]

During these years of wandering Maurin's ties with the Church were tenuous, but when queried on the subject, he would only remark that he was not living then as a Christian should. Over the years this statement remained an enigma. Did he mean that he was not attending Mass daily as he would later do, or even weekly? Or did he feel himself inattentive to the obligation that faith demanded of the person to serve one's neighbor? It is possible that Maurin was referring to his affluence in relation to the call he would later receive to live a life of poverty. Undoubtedly tied to this feeling of being outside the Church was Maurin's enjoyment of the fruits of a social order he would soon reject.[5]

Despite Maurin's inattention to matters of faith, these years of wandering were not barren of intellectual and religious search. Indeed, Maurin's vocation as a Catholic agitator, still in the future, may have germinated during these years. His move from France to Canada and now to America, in providing distance from his culture and formative religious experiences as a peasant, Christian Brother, and member of *Sillon*, caused both crisis and reflection. Where, and in what role, was Maurin to find his place in the Catholic tradition? This had not been an easy question for him to resolve, but if there was anything he could not shake in his wanderings it was the thought that he had a calling to a religious vocation.

Maurin was not alone in this search for vocation. The war itself had unsettled an entire generation of intellectuals and was, for many, to clarify the intuitive fears they held as to the direction of world history. Since his birth the world had changed considerably and, from Maurin's point of view, for the worse. Urbanism and industrialism had grown exponentially and tied to both were the growth of the state and the rise of nationalism. Ideologically this growth would take different forms, capitalism, state socialism, and eventually fascism, but the result would be the same in the increasing secularization of life and the organization of the institutional and personal spheres. Maurin was beginning to see this as a march toward totalitarianism. A world experimenting with systems of domination could do little but crush under foot the memories that asserted the value of the spirit and the person: the voice of tradition. For Maurin the power of modernity and the end of tradition seemed to be hurtling the world into darkness. It was the voice of tradition that would illumine this darkness by providing cultural continuity to the Western world, by critiquing the present, and finally by forming the basis for a new social order.

Maurin was forty-eight years old when, in 1925, he accepted a student's invitation to come to New York to teach French. What precipitated this decision is unknown, but he decided to stay in the East and the following year another student organized a class for him in Woodstock, New York. Maurin was to reside in Woodstock for the next several years, giving French lessons as a means of support. These lessons were given at the homes of his pupils, who recalled Maurin as dignified and formal. One day without notice, however, Maurin stopped charging for lessons and offered them to students saying they could pay him what they thought the lessons were worth. Perhaps the reason for this change was the idea, gleaned from reading the life of Saint Francis of Assisi, that labor ought to be given as a gift. Maurin recalled that a world in search of affluence and security had gone crazy, and he decided to be crazy in his own way by adopting a life of poverty and dependence on others. His generosity was not misplaced: "They didn't let me starve," Maurin said, and a librarian in Woodstock, Alice Thompson, allowed him to live in her barn.[6]

Julia Leaycraft, a student of Maurin's at the time, interested in Hindu thought and Gandhi, recalled that Maurin brought poems to her French lessons in a small looseleaf notebook, which undoubtedly contained some of the essays Maurin was to use in his talks to clubs and gatherings in upstate New York. The style Maurin developed was interesting. Words were grouped into phrased sentences with the object being to articulate ideas in ways accessible to the educated and uneducated alike. Having come to English as a second language, Maurin was especially interested in slogans and expressions that would catch the ear of an audience. He would read these essays to Leaycraft and ask for her comments. Leaycraft recalled that Maurin did not want to publish what he wrote, for that crystallized what should be open to the further clarification that came through the personal exchange of ideas. A year after she met Maurin, he began talking about the "Green Revolution" and how he wanted to reverse the urbanism and industrialism of contemporary life by bringing people back to the land and crafts. In Leaycraft's view this had been precipitated by the offer of a farm to Maurin by a local banker. But she also sensed something deeper than the immediacy of such an offer occurring within him. She had the impression that Maurin was a man feeling his way toward a practicing philosophy.

Maurin went frequently to Kingston, a small city ten miles from Woodstock, where he would eat at a luncheon counter under the railroad viaduct. Hoboes gathered there, often asking for meals. Maurin put a box up on the wall and appended this sign: "If you have money to give, put it in, and if you need money take it out. No one will know." His experiment had its ups and downs, with twenty-five dollars disappearing from the box, then reappearing several weeks later with a note that it had been used for bus fare. Maurin considered this a triumph for his conviction that people were essentially honest.[7]

Maurin was gaining an increasing audience for his ideas and in 1927 he was invited to speak at a Rotary Club luncheon in Kingston. Here he delivered one of the poems Julia Leaycraft had referred to, later to be a part of his "Easy Essays." The title was "The Fallacy of Saving," and the essay was an exploration of a book by the same title published in 1892 by John Robertson. Maurin told the Rotarians that they as businessmen thought they had discovered the secret of mass distribution and mass production; that "the day had come for a two-car garage, a chicken in every pot, and a sign 'To Let' in front of every poorhouse." But there was a fallacy in this premise, for saving money led to increased investment and production, which in turn led to a surplus in production, creating unemployment. The result was, as Maurin phrased it, "a great boom was built which was bound to be followed by a great depression." Pope Leo XIII in his encyclical *The Conditions of Labor* had forewarned of this, as had John Robertson. Now Maurin was saying it. But, as he recalled later, they preferred to let disturbing prophets talk in the wilderness and listened to Coolidge instead.[8]

During this time Father Joseph B. Scully opened a summer camp for children at Mount Tremper in the town of Phoenicia, five miles from Woodstock. After a series of meetings between Father Scully and Maurin, a mutual respect developed that over the years became a strong friendship. Maurin worked at the camp for the next five years as a handyman in return for food and lodging, living in a room above a stable where some horses were quartered. But Father Scully was as interested in Maurin's vocation as in his work around the camp. Scully supported his newfound mission, allowing Maurin to come and go as he pleased while providing for his expenses.[9]

Though not fully clarified, the ideas Maurin had been reflecting on about the place of the person in contemporary life and the effect of the social order on the person were now slowly evolving into a program of action. In general, the plan had the ingredients of responsibility to the needy as well as the desire to apply the social teachings of the Church to contemporary life. Attempting to find someone to take up the plan, Maurin visited priests and editors and proposed his ideas to the directors of the Third Order of Saint Francis and the Franciscan Order itself. All those who could have given Maurin a wider base of support declined to participate in his undertaking.[10]

Maurin was understandably disturbed by the Franciscans' reluctance to act. He had found the Third Order to be effective in the Harmel spinning plant in France and his hopes for their activity had been reinforced by his reading of the papal encyclicals on Francis. In one of his essays, "The Third Order of St. Francis of Assisi," Maurin quoted from the encyclicals of popes Leo XIII, Pius X, and Benedict XV on Francis and the need for the Third Order to act; their action would create order in a world plunging into chaos. But the Third Order and the Franciscan Order that Maurin approached had done little to facilitate social change. To Maurin's query, the Orders contended that they could do nothing in the social realm without being asked by the bishops; the bishops replied that they and the Orders did not know how to go about social reform. Thus, in Maurin's view, a cycle of paralysis had made ineffectual Orders that held the potential for leadership in social reform.[11]

Unable to find those who would listen within the hierarchy of the Church, Maurin turned to the outcasts in Union Square and Columbus Circle, where he would listen and speak to the unemployed and the radicals gathered there. His method was different from that of other speakers. He did not employ a soapbox, but would begin speaking to a person in the crowd in a voice loud enough to attract others. Having aroused their interest, he would analyze the evils of the present situation in the light of Church positions. In order to be in the city to speak with people, he commuted between Mount Tremper and New York City on the night boat between Kingston and New York. When he came to the city, Maurin would stay overnight at Uncle Sam's Hotel on the corner of Bowery and Houston streets for forty cents a night. Because he often gave up his bed to another in greater need than himself, Maurin spent many of these nights in coffeehouses or in parks.[12]

Maurin's newfound street ministry was developing. When

he could not find people to listen, he wrote his ideas out in neatly lettered script, duplicated them as leaflets, and distributed them on street corners. A young fallen-away Catholic took some of Maurin's essays, printed them, and handed them out as Maurin spoke. On Fifteenth Street, around the corner from Tammany Hall, a group would gather together after his talks and converse until midnight. He would then either leave for Mount Tremper or stay overnight in the city.

Maurin continued to search for someone to implement his program and in this search visited professors and editors in New York City. One of the editors with whom Maurin became friendly was George Shuster, then editor of *Commonweal*. Shuster's advice was that he seek out Dorothy Day, a journalist and recent Catholic convert, and propose his program to her. To prepare for this meeting, Maurin read articles she had written for *America* and *Commonweal*. Their meeting took place in December 1932.[13]

Dorothy Day was as important to Maurin in that bleak December as she was to be to subsequent generations of Catholics who yearned for a new dynamic in their faith. Dorothy listened to Maurin, a more arduous task than one might suppose. Though by now fluent in English, Maurin still spoke with a heavy French accent, and his technique was to engage in persistent, lengthy discourses. Despite such obstacles, Dorothy understood Maurin's message, and together they transformed his vision into reality with the start of a newspaper and the opening of a house of hospitality.

It was in these ways that Maurin's name and thought reached a growing audience emerging from the confines of Union Square to encompass a national and international hearing. Dorothy Day was to mean other things to Maurin as well; she was to be a friend and an inspiration. The conjunction of their ideas and vision was not happenstance, for if Maurin had wandered and searched and come to conclusions, so had Dorothy. Though their life experiences had been quite different, the road they were now to travel together would be the same.

Born on November 8, 1897, at Bath Beach, Brooklyn, Dorothy later characterized her childhood as protected, even though her father, a newspaperman of modest income, was forced more than once to reestablish himself and the family in different cities. She spent her teenage years in Chicago, entering the University of Illinois at Urbana in the fall of 1914. Dorothy never took to college life, for the formalities of academic discipline meant little to her. Consequently, she left college two years later for New York, where her father was racing editor for the *Morning Telegraph.* After some searching, Dorothy found a job as a reporter for the socialist *Call* and took a room in the predominantly Jewish Lower East Side.[14]

Dorothy's experiences were varied and the environment of the Lower East Side and Greenwich Village was exciting. Leaving the *Call* in April 1917 she then worked for the radical paper *The Masses* and its successor *The Liberator;* she engaged in social activism that included picketing the White House and being imprisoned with a group of militant suffragettes; she was purportedly engaged to Mike Gold, later editor of the *Daily Worker,* and became friends with Eugene O'Neill. But what seemed to be an exciting existence of interesting people and radical causes was clouded by a hidden side of lost relationships and loneliness, which she recorded in her first book, *The Eleventh Virgin,* published in the spring of 1924. In the summer that followed, Dorothy entered into a common-law relationship with Forster Batterham, an anarchist by temperament. Later she became pregnant, giving birth to a girl, Tamar, in March 1927. It was the birth of Tamar and a deepening sense of the spirit that brought Dorothy into the Catholic Church in December of the following year, an experience that caused much reflection.

> I had no particular joy in partaking of these three sacraments, Baptism, Penance and Holy Eucharist. I proceeded about my own active participation in them grimly, coldly, making acts of faith, and certainly with no consolation whatever. One part of my mind stood at one side and kept saying, "What are you doing? Are you sure of yourself? What kind of affectation is this? What act is this you are going through? Are you trying to induce emotion, induce faith, partake of an opiate, the opiate of the people?" I felt like a hypocrite if I got down on my knees, and shuddered at the thought of anyone seeing me.

I was just as much against capitalism and imperialism as ever, and here I was going over to the opposition, because of course the Church was lined up with property, with the wealthy, with the state, with capitalism, with all the forces of reaction.... I certainy believed this, but I wanted to be poor, chaste and obedient. I wanted to die in order to live, to put off the old man and put on Christ. I loved, in other words, and like all women in love, I wanted to be united to my love.

I loved the Church for Christ made visible. Not for itself, because it was so often a scandal to me.[15]

The years that followed were permeated with uncertainty. Because of her entrance into the Church, she terminated her relationship with Forster and was on her own where the problem of supporting Tamar was concerned. She was again drawn to writing and was offered a job in Hollywood writing movie scripts, a position she gladly accepted. Three months later, after a mutually unsatisfactory experience, Dorothy left Hollywood for Mexico City, where expenses were low and she could live from the income she received from articles she wrote for *Commonweal*. Tamar, though, suffered from a chronic digestive disorder, and in May 1930 Dorothy returned to New York, where she settled into a library research job for the next two years. Then in December 1932, with the urging of friends, she covered the "hunger march" in Washington, D.C., an event that was to change her life.

The march in Washington was a gathering of thousands of those who had been engulfed by the spreading depression, and reawakened Dorothy's desire to be with and work for the unemployed and the poor as she had done in her earlier days as a socialist. In Dorothy's view, they were Christ's poor as Christ was a man like other men, and had chosen his friends among ordinary workers. To Dorothy, these hungry ragged ones had been betrayed by a Christianity unwilling to fulfill its calling. On reflecting on the unemployed and the poor she found herself in a dilemma:

I felt that they were my people, that I was part of them. I had worked for them and with them in the past, and now I was a Catholic and could not be a communist. I could not join this united front of protest and I wanted to.[16]

The next day, December 8, on the Feast of the Immaculate Conception and at the Shrine of the Immaculate Conception, Dorothy offered a prayer that a way would be shown for her to affirm the spiritual reality of God in the process of history by working for the poor and the oppressed.

On Dorothy's return to her apartment at 416 East Fifteenth Street, a four-room railroad apartment in an old five-story tenement that she shared with her daughter and her brother and sister-in-law, she found Maurin waiting for her. Actually he had arrived several days before in search of Dorothy. Finding her away, Maurin began talking with Tessa, Dorothy's sister-in-law.

His appearance was uncommon by normal social standards yet certainly common for the simplicity that characterized his life. He was short, stockily built, garbed in thick heavy-soled shoes, a khaki shirt, and shabby stained pants. The pockets of his overcoat were crammed with books and papers. His glasses, with one earpiece missing, were bought along the Bowery. But more must have seemed uncommon to Tessa than Maurin's appearance. His conversation had become almost a monologue that would continue uninterrupted until his point had been made, though when finished he would listen to another's ideas without interruption. This "technique of agitation," as it would later be called, included uncommon subjects as well: Church history, the saints, and the role of the laity in changing the social order. To the uninitiated person this must have sounded strange indeed.

If anything, Maurin was persistent, and he returned several days later. Tessa advised him that Dorothy was still in Washington and no sooner had she said this than Maurin recited an essay he had written in previous days.

SELF-ORGANIZATION

People go to Washington
asking the Federal Government
to solve their economic problems,

while the Federal Government
was never intended
to solve men's economic problems.
Thomas Jefferson says that
the less government there is,
the better it is.
If the less government there is,
the better it is,
then the best kind of government
is self-government.
If the best kind of government
is self-government,
then the best kind of organization
is self-organization.
When the organizers try
to organize the unorganized,
then the organizers
don't organize themselves.
And when the organizers
don't organize themselves,
nobody organizes himself.
And when nobody organizes himself,
nothing is organized.[17]

In Maurin's view, Dorothy had misperceived the locus of power, placing it in centralized political organization rather than in local, personal activity. Maurin's mission was to convince her of this and he was beginning to realize the difficulties involved.

Several days later Dorothy returned, as did Maurin, and a routine ensued that was to become the foundation of their relationship. Every day for the next four months Maurin came to Dorothy's apartment and talked to her from three in the afternoon to eleven at night until, finally exhausted from it all, she would turn him out. Sometimes he brought friends, once including an itinerant sculptor and a musician who played the flute as Maurin talked. Maurin would follow Dorothy as she moved around the house, giving her a history of the Church and interpreting contemporary events in the light of that history. In his daily visits he would bring her books on the lives of the saints and the tradition of the Church, books he felt important for Dorothy's intellectual and spiritual development.

Maurin also presented Dorothy with a written digest (essentially selected passages arranged in Maurin's essay format) of Peter Kropotkin's *Field, Factories, and Workshops* (1889), a book to which he had been introduced in his last years in France. Kropotkin was a late nineteenth-century anarchist and biologist who lived in an age that stressed the efficacy of struggle and competition. But from his own studies of peasant societies Kropotkin concluded the opposite: Rather than competition, the principles of cooperation and mutual aid were the natural and most efficient tendencies of humankind.

Maurin had come to the same conclusions. The ideas of Kropotkin's that were important to Maurin are illustrated by his selection of essay headings, including the division of labor, regional economy, the possibility of agriculture, and small industries and industrial villages. The arguments contained in these essays were simple and direct, predicated on the contention that specialization of labor had divided the community into classes and, with the triumph of industry, had destroyed the village and separated the people from the land. The result was alienation and the demise of skilled labor. This was a process that capitalism encouraged because it was exploitative and prevented the blending of the small factory with the village, a blending that would have retained the customs of the village and allowed it to survive. Moreover, the destruction of the village signaled the end of traditional values and culture with their emphasis on religion and community.[18]

For Maurin, though, critique was not enough. He reminded Dorothy over and over again of the necessity for the institution of his program of action, which had now crystallized. At the center of this program were to be round-table discussions where thought would be clarified, houses of hospitality where the needy would be served, and "agronomic" universities where people going back to the land would receive training. With Dorothy's journalistic background, Maurin proposed that she publish a paper publicizing these theories and programs. How would they start? Though Maurin would only enunciate the principles, he told her to look for practical guidance from the saints. "In the history of the saints capital was raised by prayer," he told Dorothy; "God sends you what you need when you need it." Still, at the same time both Maurin and Dorothy hoped to attract benefactors.

By April, Dorothy had the necessary resources to plan an issue of a newspaper to be ready for distribution on May 1. The funds came mainly from her own earnings and included a generous payment from Father Joseph McSorley for a small bibliographical job she had recently finished. This was supplemented by small donations from a Father Ahearn and a Sister Peter Claver who worked among poor blacks in Newark. With this money Dorothy went to Paulist Press and for fifty-seven dollars ordered 2,500 copies of the paper printed. A new voice was added to the debate on America's future in the way of this small tabloid, the *Catholic Worker*, a voice that was small and poor and seemed to many to be a contradiction: Catholic *and* radical.

During the winter of 1933 Maurin continued his work at Mount Tremper, visiting New York City in February to attend a Catholic Industrial Conference at the Astor Hotel and then leaving again for the country. On April 3, Maurin wrote a letter to Dorothy using his essay style, soliciting her advice on his technique of agitation (was it too rough? did it overshoot the mark?). Returning to ideas, Maurin mentioned that three men he had talked with agreed that the basis of modern society was systematic selfishness, thus the basis of the new society had to be systematic unselfishness. The former had given us greedy corporations; the latter would bring us charitable institutions. Rousseau had said that civilization was a matter of business contracts, but Maurin thought that civilization was a matter of personal contacts. It was harmonious contacts that would make persons good to each other. The difficulty in shifting a civilization from contracts to contacts was not to be underestimated and would not be easy. If they met with some discouragement, there would also be much encouragement. In any case, Maurin said, it would be a great adventure.[19]

CHAPTER THREE

Toward a Christian
Social Order
1933–1934

As May 1933 approached, the country found itself in a deepening depression, and New York's Union Square was filled with the voices of hopeful radicals and the somber faces of the unemployed. Dorothy Day and Joe Bennett, a young Catholic convert, entered Union Square on that May Day to distribute the first issue of the *Catholic Worker*, a paper dedicated to the unemployed and the poor. The *Catholic Worker* was published to call attention to the potential social program of the Catholic Church as a sign to the unemployed and the poor that there were people of God who were working not only for their spiritual but for their material welfare.

The fundamental aim of most radical papers was the conversion of readers to a secular radicalism. The *Worker*, on the other hand, promised to confront the question that concerned many who had, at one time or another, found themselves within a faith tradition: Was it possible to be both radical and religious? Dorothy Day did not take this question lightly. "Is it not possible to protest, to expose, to complain, to point to abuses and demand reforms without desiring the overthrow of religion?" she asked. The *Worker* went beyond merely demonstrating the ability to be radical and religious, for it asserted that to be religious was to stand in the most radical position of all. In doing this the *Worker* called attention to the Church's program for the reconstruction of the social order, utilizing the papal encyclicals, especially Leo XIII's *The Condition of the Working Classes* and Pius XI's *Forty Years After* (*Quadragesimo Anno*, 1931).

As a key principle the editors decided to share more than their opinions and vision; they would share the poverty of the unemployed and the poor as well. The May issue of the *Catholic Worker* had been planned and written on the kitchen table of a tenement on Fifteenth Street, on subway platforms, and on the Staten Island ferry. There was no editorial office and the editorial work for the June issue was done on Staten Island. Overhead, therefore, was minimal and all work was voluntary rather than salaried. The money for the issues was begged and borrowed from the editors' own earnings, even to the point of letting private gas and electric bills languish. In an aside, it was noted that the utility companies had become "unwitting cooperators in the cause of social justice" for accepting delay in payment. Reflecting on their precarious existence the editors looked to the New Testament, noting that Christ wandered this earth with no place to lay his head.[1]

The first issue won anything but approval from Maurin. He had seen the proofs as they came back from the printer and felt there had been undue attention paid to the news of the day such as exploitation of blacks in the South, the abuse of child labor, and a local strike over wages and hours. It was, in Maurin's words, "everyone's paper," and everyone's paper was to him no one's paper. Obviously saddened, Maurin rose and left Dorothy Day's apartment, heading for Mount Tremper. He was not heard from for over a month.

Actually, Maurin's disappointment went beyond topic selection, for several disputes had arisen prior to publication. The name of the paper was one area of disagreement. Maurin preferred *Catholic Radical* to *Catholic Worker* because he was more interested in deep-seated social transformation than in being representative of any one group of people, such as the laboring class. Another area was the type of articles printed. Maurin perceived a format devoted less to topical discussions and more to his own essays and articles concerning faith and philosophy. On both counts, Dorothy Day's socialist background with its emphasis on the struggles of the day prevailed over Maurin's philosophical bias. While not pleased with either the name of the paper or its content, Maurin finally returned one day, repeating his statement that "everyone's paper was no one's paper," and promptly took up once again with the indoctrination of Dorothy Day. However, though he was willing to continue submitting his articles to the paper, Maurin wanted it clear that he did not necessarily advocate any particular reform carried in the pages of the newspaper. The June–July issue of the *Worker* carried this proviso: Because his program was specific and definite, Maurin would resign as an editor and sign any work he contributed. This would make it clear to readers what Maurin himself proposed.[2]

Despite these problems, several of Maurin's essays appeared on the front page of the first issue of the paper. His words held a certain intensity, particularly when they addressed the dynamic potential of the Church's message.

> Writing about the Catholic Church, a radical writer says: "Rome will have to do more than to play a waiting game; she will have to use some of the dynamic inherent in her message."
>
> To blow the dynamite of a message is the only way to make the message dynamic.
>
> If the Catholic Church is not today the dominant social, dynamic force, it is because Catholic scholars have failed to blow the dynamite of the Church.
>
> Catholic scholars have taken the dynamite of the Church, have wrapped it up in nice phraseology, placed it in an hermetic container; and sat on the lid.
>
> It is about time to blow the lid off so the Catholic Church may again become the dominant social dynamic force.[3]

To blow the dynamite of the church Maurin announced a program in the second issue of the *Catholic Worker* that, like his essays, continualy juxtaposed the present with the building of a new social order.

> My program stands for three things. Round Table Discussions, and I hope to hold the first at the Manhattan Lyceum the last Sunday of June.... I hope everybody will come to

this meeting. I want Communists, radicals, priests and laity. I want everyone to set forth his views. I want the clarification of thought.

The next step in the program is houses of hospitality. In the Middle Ages it was an obligation of the bishops to provide houses of hospitality or hospices for the wayfarer. They are especially necessary now, and necessary to my program as half-way houses. I am hoping that someone will donate a house, rent free, for six months, so that a start may be made. A priest will be at the head of it and men gathered through our round table discussions will be recruited to work in the houses cooperatively and eventually be sent out to farm colonies or agronomic universities. Which comes to the third step in my program. People will have to go back to the land. The machine has displaced labor, the cities are overcrowded. The land will have to take care of them.

My whole scheme is a utopian, Christian Communism. I am not afraid of the word communism. I am not saying that my program is for everyone. It is for those who choose to embrace it. I am not opposed to private property with responsibility. But those who own private property should never forget that it is a trust.[4]

By the summer of 1933 these three bases of Maurin's program had evolved into the central focus of the Catholic Worker movement. The first part, a call to round-table discussions for the clarification of thought, was specifically designed to move beyond cultural clichés and prejudice by bringing all elements of the community—scholar, middle-class, and worker—together. The gathering of people with diverse backgrounds, talents, and perspectives would have a beneficial effect on all involved and would provide the context for arriving at a common understanding of the present and future possibilities. The discussions were to be focused on learning the ills of the present, determining how things should be in the ideal, and, finally, discerning a path to move the social order from where it was to where it ought to be. A community setting would mitigate the divisive class and status divisions that stymied efforts to change the present. Because the scholar would be forced to confront theory with social reality, discussions would keep "trained minds from becoming academic"; because discussions would expose the worker to the ideals of the scholar, it would keep "untrained minds from becoming superficial." Though persons from the middle class figured less prominently than either scholars or workers, Maurin made it clear that the bourgeoisie would benefit from hearing the ideals of the scholar and seeing the reality of the worker. It would also lend urgency and depth to the roles of both thinker and worker, who could now assume their primary roles of guiding and implementing, with their minds and hands, a new social order.

The second part of Maurin's program was the development of houses of hospitality, an idea he derived from the Christian hospices found among early and medieval Christian communities. In these communities the stranger and the poor, the widow and the orphan, had been served by the more fortunate. The revival of these hospices could function on a variety of levels. Immediate needs of the depression years could be answered, such as the need for shelter, clothing, and food for the dispossessed. Those who came to the hospice and joined in its atmosphere of service and sacrifice would gain insight into the human costs of the present social order because they were no longer isolated from the sufferings of the unemployed and the poor, in a sense demystifying the "givenness" of the social order. Finally, hospices would serve a spiritual function, allowing the affluent opportunity to participate in their own salvation by fulfilling Christ's command to love and serve neighbor.

Service and the divine intermingled in hospitality was a central and intriguing feature of Maurin's developing thought. In his view, being with the poor and the outcast was being *with* Christ; to encounter the suffering of others was to participate in the suffering of Christ. In a profound and perhaps mysterious way, to serve those in need was to embody the message of salvation that Christ had preached. This encounter could not help but raise the radical question of whom one was going to serve: the divine or the material.

The development of what Maurin called "agronomic universities" was the third part of his program and was perhaps the most controversial, for its implementation was delayed for several years and remained ever problematic. Agronomic universities, later to be called farming communes, were to be centers located in the country to train urban dwellers in the methods of farming and crafts. This training and the formation of farming cooperatives would eventually pave the way for a general return to the land and a village way of life.

Typically, there were several levels to Maurin's proposal. Farming communes would fulfill the immediate needs of people in the depression years by providing free rent, fuel, and food, which, while artificially scarce in the city, were naturally abundant in the country. A return to the land would mitigate the technological and cyclical unemployment Maurin thought inherent in an industrial economy, contributing to a more stable and just social order. Moreover, subsistence farming and crafts would direct the forces of production once again to need rather than profit, and so provide a basis for the recovery of the values of cooperation and the spiritual dimensions of human existence. With its emphasis on community and spirit, Maurin thought that farming and crafts would produce the highest culture possible, and later he equated the return to the land with the return to Christ.[5]

The implementation of Maurin's proposal for round-table discussions began in the summer of 1933. He had secured the Manhattan Lyceum on East Fourth Street, which was a traditional gathering place for radicals and the unemployed. The first meeting was scheduled to be held in June and Maurin enumerated the advantages of this initial location: The cost was low—ten dollars for eight hours—and the hall could hold 150 people. He had paid a deposit of three dollars and, being without funds, hoped to beg the rest. Maurin's invitation to the discussion was wide ranging and provocative, providing a framework for the discussion itself. Having invited priests, laity, and radicals, Maurin laid out his scheme. To a commercial industrial economy he was proposing a cultural agrarian economy. To systematic selfishness he was proposing systematic unselfishness. To the sociology of Karl Marx, Lenin, and Stalin he was proposing the sociology of Francis of Assisi and Leon Harmel. And to dictatorial pagan communism he was proposing utopian Christian communism. Though this was his own undertaking, there would be no discrimination and Maurin invited all to set forth their views so as to reach a clarification of thought.[6]

This first meeting, held on the last Sunday of June, was acclaimed by the *Catholic Worker* to be a success though only fifteen people attended. Clarification of thought was facilitated by the presence of a few communists who, because of their attack on Church piety as a barrier to social change, forced Catholics to analyze and articulate the Church's program for social reconstruction. To a speaker who claimed that the Church and the capitalist system were inextricably bound together, the members of the audience, no doubt with the prompting of Maurin, cited the Christian communism of the early Church, the guild system of the Middle Ages, and the examples of Saint Francis of Assisi and Leon Harmel. Maurin addressed the meeting, speaking of the Church's reasons for the condemnation of nineteenth-century liberalism, the primary one being affirmation of the separation of the religious and secular realms. He also cited the growing division between the bishops and the laity as a problem in need of resolution, especially if Catholics were to act in concert to reform the social order.[7]

The second round-table discussion was held on the last Sunday of July and was equally successful, though not without incidence. When Maurin went to Union Square to publicize the meeting, a communist seized copies of the paper he was distributing. In the ensuing struggle Maurin's leather briefcase was torn apart but the papers were saved. Despite the incident and the oppressive heat of summer, the meeting was well attended. Though still commuting from Mount Tremper, Maurin conducted the discussion and spoke on the reconstruction of the social order, emphasizing its importance and expressing concern that there was too much talk of patching up a system that was contrary to Christian ethics. An important presence at the meeting was the Jesuit Father John LaFarge, coeditor of *America* and head of the Laymen's Union for Negro Catholics. He was the first priest to attend the discussions, and his positive opinion of Maurin and the session lent a greater immediacy to Maurin's agitation. Father LaFarge told Maurin he would urge his black friends to attnd the meeting on September 9, a meeting specifically called to draw up plans for immediate relief for the victims of the depression.[8]

The meeting of bishops and archbishops at the National Conference of Catholic Charities in New York provided the framework for the third round-table discussion and produced a plea from Maurin to the bishops of the United States for the opening of houses of hospitality throughout the nation. This plea was published in the October issue of the *Catholic Worker* as an open letter. Maurin began by recalling the duty of Christians to accord hospitality.

THE DUTY OF HOSPITALITY

1. People who are in need
   and are not afraid to beg
   give to people not in need
   the occasion to do good
   for goodness' sake.
2. Modern society calls the beggar
   bum and panhandler
   and gives him the bum's rush.
3. But the Greeks used to say
   that the people in need are the ambassadors of the gods.
4. Although you may be called
   bums and panhandlers,
   you are in fact the Ambassadors of God.
5. As God's Ambassadors
   you should be given food,
   clothing and shelter
   by those who are able to give it.
6. Mahometan teachers tell us
   that God commands hospitality.
7. And hospitality is still practiced
   in Mahometan countries.
8. But the duty of hospitality
   is neither taught nor practiced
   in Christian countries.[9]

To Maurin this was a paradox. During the early ages of Christianity the hospice was a shelter for the sick, the poor, the orphans, and the needy of every kind. These hospices were under the supervision of bishops, who designated priests to administer them. Maurin lamented that now the unemployed were sent to the municipal shelter, where hospitality came from the taxpayer's pocketbook rather than from the heart. This was a perversion of hospitality for, like everything else, hospitality had become commercialized. The development of houses of hospitality would reverse this trend toward commercialization and abdication of personal responsibility. Toward this end, Maurin suggested to the bishops that houses of hospitality be established in every parish and that rooms for hospitality be available in every home.

The fruits of these hospices would be many. The rich would be given the opportunity to serve the poor, thus participating in their own salvation. The administration of the hospices would bring both the hierarchy and the laity into contact with the social order and each other, truly bringing the bishops to the people and the people to the bishops. The world would see what idealism looked like in practice as the technique of institutions, that is, the extension of personal responsibility into the public realm, would be recovered to institutions. Moreover, houses of hospitality would be more than free guest houses for the unemployed, for they would also provide the context for round-table discussions and religious instruction and become vocational training schools, including training for the priesthood, and Catholic reading rooms.[10]

Maurin's pleas for hospitality drew no response from the bishops but a month later inspired the opening of the Teresa-Joseph Cooperative, an apartment in the parish of the Immaculate Conception, which housed ten homeless women. In an article published in the December issue of the *Catholic Worker*, Maurin was given credit for the house, inspired as it was by his "constant propaganda" for personal responsibility and hospitality among Catholics. This was a small beginning to be sure, but the streets of the city were cold in the winter and the homeless abounded. Beds were in short supply and the people at Teresa-Joseph borrowed blankets, often donated by those who worked on the *Worker*. Some of the women who came to the hospice were kept warm with newspapers and rugs. This was the first of many houses of hospitality that had its impetus in Maurin's thought and that, by the late 1930s, were present in locations all around the country.[11]

In February 1934 Maurin announced a new venture in round-table discussions in the form of the Catholic Worker School. This was a project that testified both to Maurin's confidence in the role of discussion and to the zeal of a movement just born. The purpose of the school was to bring Catholic thought to Catholic laborers in preparation for action in a Catholic context. The program was diverse, with topics ranging from scholastic philosophy to liturgical arts, and showed the extent of Maurin's connections in academic and Church circles. Many of the people who spoke at the school were well known, such as Carlton Hayes of Columbia University, Ross Hoffman of New York University, Father Wilfred Parsons, editor of *America*, Father Joseph McSorley, a Paulist priest and Dorothy Day's confessor, and Monsignor John A. Ryan, who was head of the Social Action Department of Catholic University. Meetings were held nightly beginning in February and ran almost every night of the week for the next several years.[12]

The opening was exciting as the lecture attracted people from diverse ethnic and economic backgrounds with blacks, Jews, Germans, and Russians, the unemployed, workers, and students attending. Carlton Hayes began the series of lectures with a talk on nationalism. In Hayes's view, the growth of nationalism made the pursuit of rational social reform impossible because it fomented racial and religious intolerance. People, he suggested, could work toward a profound and radical reform of capitalism if some limit were set on the absolute sovereignty of the state. Maurin reflected on this talk with a short essay entitled "My Country, Right or Wrong."

> To stand up for one's country
> when one's country is wrong
> does not make the country right.
>
> To stand up for the right
> even when the world is wrong
> is the only way we know of
> to make everything right.[13]

TOWARD A CHRISTIAN SOCIAL ORDER

Professor L. B. Holsapple contributed to the discussion in a comparison of medieval times with the present. It was Holsapple's belief that in the Middle Ages the Church and state embraced all people, leading to a unity of thought. But the present saw no such unity and Holsapple concluded that modern nationalism signaled a move back to the idea of the Greek city states, with armed camps poised against each other. One way to remedy this situation was to study the ideals of the Middle Ages, yet without idealizing the period itself. To this Maurin responded with an essay entitled "From High Ethics to No Ethics."

> When Thorsten Veblen published
> "The Theory of the Leisure Class" in 1899
> students in economics began to realize
> that there are no ethics in modern society.
>
> R. H. Tawney, an Oxford student,
> learned that there were high ethics in society
> when the Canon Law was the law of the land—
>
> How society has gone down
>   from the high ethics of the Canon Law
>   —that is to say the Law of the Church—
>   to the no ethics of to-day
>   is embodied in R. H. Tawney's book
>   "Religion and the Rise of Capitalism."[14]

The urgency of Maurin's program evolved around a deepening economic depression but also, by the winter of 1934, around a now articulate critique of modern economics. Maurin phrased the economic problem in stages and in simple but insightful terms. Following a thousand-year tradition in the Church and citing the analysis of R. H. Tawney, then a medieval historian at Oxford, Maurin placed legalized moneylending at interest as the center of the economic malaise. According to Maurin, lending at interest allowed people to live off "the sweat of another's brow," that is, to profit from another's labor. It was also a way of reaping profits on property without assuming the responsibility of property, thus encouraging absentee ownership of tenements and land.

The mortgaging of everything from homes to government budgets was another result of lending at interest, and because of this the profit motive had been instilled into every aspect of life. Churches were mortgaged, too, and Maurin thought that such a travesty decreased the ability of the faithful to do as Jesus had done in defense of the poor and the sacred: drive the moneylenders out of the Temple. In effect, being tied to a system of borrowing and repayment decreased the ability of the populace and the Church to challenge the social order. The result was a paralysis of economic and religious life. Maurin declared that mortgaging had become a "veritable octopus strangling the life of our people." To break this cycle, Maurin suggested that two laws be implemented immediately. The first would make all moneylending at interest illegal; the second would oblige money borrowers to pay the lenders 1 percent of the capital every year until the loan was repaid, thus lightening the burden of the money borrowers without robbing the moneylenders.[15]

The lending of money at interest, however, went beyond economic matters in its significance, and Maurin spent many of his nights in Union Square addressing this problem. To garner wealth, people ceased to produce for use and began to produce for profit. Values changed because a society concerned with profit emphasized competition over cooperation and rewarded the "rugged individualist" rather than the "gentle personalist." A society concerned with profit was an acquisitive society and the accumulation of goods was its hallmark. Citizens once interested in the public realm became consumers nurturing private consumption. The result was that the bank account had become the standard of values.[16]

Though Maurin's sketch here might be broad, it contains an essential critique of modern society with its attempt, at least theoretically, to divorce culture from economy. In Maurin's view, a society fulfilling an inner dynamic based on profit and materialism could lead only to its own consumption and ultimate destruction, for the religious and community values that helped shape tradition and the history of peoples were being split asunder by the pursuit of the material. Without an ethical and ultimately religious structure that could place economy in its proper perspective, the result would be the demise of culture, even of civilization itself.

Economic revitalization programs offered to Americans as the hope of the future, such as Roosevelt's New Deal, left Maurin unimpressed. That program did not address the problems he saw as fundamental, the problems of moneylending at interest, which continued the cycle of inflation and unemployment, and ethical subservience to the motive of profit. Maurin characterized the New Deal as "Roosevelt's experiment," saw its method as erratic, and viewed the president as merely "muddling through."[17]

While Maurin rarely mentioned any of Roosevelt's programs directly, when he did he was critical. The National Recovery Administration (NRA) of 1933 stood as an example of what he saw as the dilemma of the New Deal. As passed, NRA had a dual purpose of recovery and reform. It was designed to speed up industrial production, raise wages, and provide money for public works and emergency relief, while at the same time it proposed new safeguards for labor rights and reduced the waste of competition, thus encouraging monopolies. Maurin depicted NRA as a horse pulling in two directions, with the head of the horse standing for recovery and the tail of the horse for reformation. The effect was that neither recovery nor reform was accomplished.

NRA evidenced to Maurin an American "bureaucratic failure," a theme that became central to his understanding of the Roosevelt years and the twentieth century in general. Though Maurin did not elaborate on the specifics of the bureaucratic failure of NRA, he did discuss the problem of bureaucracy in relation to Europe as a warning to America. Though governments changed, bureaucracy remained, encouraging political corruption and apathy. To illustrate his point, Maurin used two examples. The first was France, where bureaucratic corruption and the inability of elected officials to discipline the bureaucracy had produced a people disgruntled with their political process. Germany was the second example. In Germany the bureaucracy was so efficient that the people failed to create a climate for democratic politics, allowing the Nazis to mobilize the public sector in an authoritarian manner. Whether in commercialized charity or undemocratic politics, Maurin thought bureaucracy usurped the role of personal responsibility, and its excesses encouraged cynicism and totalitarianism.[18]

The problems of the New Deal, however, were more than misguided economic policies and an entrenched bureaucracy. According to Maurin, the fundamental problem was that Roosevelt's brain trust was comprised of pragmatists working in the superficial arena of the economy rather than idealists going to the root of economic theory. One night at dinner Maurin exclaimed:

> The NRA is pragmatism in politics. Experimentation without theory is back of it. Let's try—let's try! Bump your head against the wall and then find it's hard. Try everything but the door—and only then the door. First the FRC, then the NRA, the AAA, CCC, PWA, CWA, FERA, and now it's no longer emergency administration, but rehabilitation—one foot on the land—the other on industry. Attempting something without trying to get at the root of things.[19]

Maurin advised that economists would do better to go back to thinkers who addressed the foundations of economy because they began with the person and his relationship with God, thus deriving the social and economic order from the standpoint of the person rather than profit. Accordingly he suggested that the New Dealers should go back to Aristotle and from there to Thomas Aquinas.[20]

Maurin's analysis and rejection of a profit-oriented economy, which he identified with capitalism, led him to refute with equal force its most vocal enemy, Marxism, which he believed had evolved into state socialism. Both ideologies were similar in that they saw the organization of the material world as the messianic element in history. Capitalism viewed the material world as an avenue to individual satisfaction; state socialism considered materialism the sole arena in which economic justice could be achieved. To reach their respective ends both sought the elimination of spiritual values. Their institutions were further evidence of the similarities between the two because, for all intents and purposes, capitalist and socialist economies had the same structures of industry, wages, and bureaucracy. Furthermore, Maurin thought that state socialism had sprung from the failure of capitalism in that the irresponsible use of wealth had aroused resentment against a system of greed and exploitation. But though state socialism was an advancement in its recognition that the pauperization of workers attendant to the rise of the capitalist economic system had to end, it sought only a restitution of goods and social equality. For Maurin, the basis of exploitation in industrial labor and the concomitant lack of spiritual values were not addressed by state socialism.[21]

Though he rejected the state socialism of his day, Maurin embraced wholeheartedly the communism of Christianity, especially the communism of the early Christians and the monasteries. He made much of distinguishing state socialism and Christian communism, seeing the former built on the materialistic forces of historical determinism and class warfare, the latter on the spiritual dimensions of faith and service. If state socialism was another guise for the pursuit of affluence, Christian communism emphasized sacrifice and renunciation. State socialism was characterized by polarization and coercion; Christian communism by free choice and love. The differences were clear and important. Socialism was diametrically opposed to Catholicism because it was essentially materialist in aims and left out entirely the beginning and the end of life, which was God.[22]

By positing his utopian Christian view against the present economic systems of capitalism and state socialism, Maurin raised significant theoretical questions that went beyond the economy itself. In a profound way Maurin was opening up the question of human freedom and responsibility. What was the basis of freedom? Was it affluence, even a justly apportioned affluence, or was it seeking the spiritual dimensions of existence? Did pursuit of the material, and the ease that came from its achievement, provide the context for personal meaning, or did the attention paid to the material close off that which came in humility and prayer? There was also the question of responsibility. Did addressing persons in institutional frameworks, a necessity in both capitalism and state socialism, provide the care and concern that would assure the person a meaningful place in the community?

Maurin's taste for agitation and search for clarification were hardly quenched by the round-table discussions at the Manhattan Lyceum and the opening of the Catholic Worker School or by his essays on the economy. In October 1933, prompted by correspondence published in the *Catholic Worker* with Father Daniel Lord, S.J., professor of theology at St. Louis University, Maurin gradually developed a concept central to his social program. He addressed the words to a discontented world beginning to realize that things are not good enough to be left alone. The work Father Lord did among Catholic college youth was in Maurin's view important though limited, because his students were only a fraction of Catholic youth and then only a fraction of youth in general. Maurin wondered about the audience Lord was missing, those who had reached the age of maturity without having reached the "state of maturity," for they needed him as much as did Catholic college youth. To help spread Father Lord's work among the masses, Maurin suggested starting at St. Louis University a school of Catholic Agitation for the popularization of Catholic Action.[23]

In the December 1933 issue of the *Catholic Worker* Maurin published a second open letter to Father Lord concerning discussions in which he had participated regarding the social value of fascism. In this letter Maurin analyzed the rising tide of fascism as only a stopgap between the rugged individualism of capitalism and the rugged collectivism of state socialism. There were no essential differences between fascist or communist dictatorships, for the trouble, he said, was simply too much dictatorship and not enough leadership. Surely leadership could not be found among politicians or businessmen, but leadership *could* be found among the "appointed leaders of mankind," the Catholic bishops. That Catholic laymen and women looked to the bishops for spiritual teaching but looked to politicians and businessmen in political and economic matters was a tragedy that militated against the possibility of religious leadership and, according to Maurin, increased the propensity toward secular dictatorship. To relegate authority to secular leaders was to commit the great modern error of separating the spiritual and the material, which Maurin, like Pius XI, called the modern plague of secularism. To help in the rebirth of the proper understanding of authority, Maurin appealed to Lord to bring a thorough understanding among bishops, clergy, and lay people. From that understanding would spring a dynamic Catholic faith, so dynamic as to eliminate the lure of communist and fascist appeals.[24]

As his correspondence with Father Lord indicated, the term "Catholic Action," which had been used for some years in papal encyclicals, was becoming more and more prominent in Maurin's vocabulary and thought. To many, however, the term was new and ambiguous. In its broadest terms, Catholic Action had as its primary goal the reconstruction of the social order so as to reassert the primacy of the spiritual in the personal and social realms. By extension, this envisioned the reentry of the Church into the process of shaping culture and society.

For Maurin, Catholic Action began with the recognition of the validity of the Catholic spiritual and intellectual tradition. It thus inevitably began with faith and the implications of that faith.

> The central act of devotional life
> in the Catholic Church
> is the Holy Sacrifice of the Mass.
> The Sacrifice of the Mass
> is the unbloody repetition
> of the sacrifice of the Cross.
> On the Cross of Calvary
> Christ gave his life to redeem the world.
> The life of Christ was a life of sacrifice.
> The life of a Christian must be
> a life of sacrifice.
> We cannot imitate the sacrifice of Christ
> on Calvary
> by trying to get all we can.

PETER MAURIN

We can only imitate the sacrifice of Christ
on Calvary
by trying to give all we can.[25]

That Christ sacrificed his life to redeem the world was instructive, and to follow Christ was to lead a life of sacrifice. This following of Christ transformed one's view of self and neighbor. With this transformative faith, Maurin, taking a hint from Thomas Aquinas, could no longer see the person as an individual with individual rights, but instead as a "person with personal duties toward God, himself and his fellow man." As a person one could not serve God without serving the common good. Social relations, therefore, were to be governed from the standpoint of a new relationship, the relationship of faith and obligation.[26]

If faith and obligation were the foundations of Catholic Action, its ends were for Maurin equally clear. Christ would be the leader and the standard of values would be the Sermon on the Mount. The priest would be the mediator and the educator would train the minds of pupils so they could understand the message of the priest. Politicians would assure law and order according to the priest's teachings. Technicians would devise a system for the just production and distribution of goods, and the administrator would administer according to directions from technicians. With Christ as leader there would be a functional rather than an acquisitive society.

Between the foundations of faith and this future society lay the difficult task of translating ideals into reality. This was the task of Catholic Action, a task Maurin referred to alternately as creating order out of chaos and giving birth to a new social order. Such had been attempted before by the gathering of Christians in community, and Maurin in his talks and essays often pointed out the present possibilities of Catholic Action by reference to the past.

The first Christians served as one of these references for Maurin. Though persecuted, they testified to their belief in Jesus and eventually contributed to social reform through the daily practice of the seven corporal and seven spiritual works of mercy. As Christ had commanded, the early Christians fed the hungry, clothed the naked, sheltered the homeless and instructed the ignorant, all at a personal sacrifice. Such sacrifice served as the unifying force of early Christian communities and as an example to the surrounding pagan culture, forcing the Romans to say of the Christians, "See how they love each other." This witness of personal sacrifice and love of neighbor played a major role in the conversion of the Roman Empire.[27]

Maurin viewed the second example of a Catholic social reconstruction as occurring hundreds of years later, when invading barbarians were met by Irish scholars and missionaries during the decline of the Roman Empire. Despite the chaos associated with the decline of Rome, the Irish laid the foundations of medieval Christendom through an intellectual synthesis and dynamic social action. This combination of thought and action intrigued Maurin. The Irish established cultural centers all over Europe where, in his words, "people could look for thought so they could have light." They opened free guest houses that popularized the virtue of charity and developed farming colonies that provided work and food for the dispossessed. This caused the Teutonic rulers to inform their people that "the Irish are good people busy doing good." Through personal charity and voluntary poverty the Irish had guided the Western world through the most difficult times and, in the process, had made the so-called Dark Ages light.[28]

A common thread was woven through these past transformations, a thread Maurin saw as instructive for the future. Foremost was the community witness of faith and charity in the midst of a decadent and dying milieu. That a community of witnesses to Christian ideals, like the first Christians or the Irish missionaries, had the ability to create order among themselves often convinced and converted the surrounding culture. As Maurin understood it, the creation of this order was achieved through the commitment to ideals and love, not through wealth, violence, or political power. Culture transformations came from below, subverting the dominant culture through personal example and perseverance. The power to witness and persevere came from faith.

Faith put at the service of culture had the effect of spiritualizing culture, and to spiritualize culture one had to use spiritual techniques. For Maurin, spiritual techniques were the use of "pure means," and so he placed pure means at the center of Catholic Action. Pure means were as simple as they were radical, for they epitomized personal action and responsibility and emphasized the spiritual over the material. Maurin quoted Jacques Maritain on the subject:

> It is not a question of changing the system, it is a question of changing the man who makes the system. It is not the temporal that creates the spiritual, it is the spiritual that creates the temporal environment.... There is no social revolution without a spiritual revolution. The trouble with radicals is not that they are too radical but not radical enough. External radicalism is not radical enough because it is external. Inner radicalism is true radicalism.[29]

Inner radicalism did not wait for political movements or societal reorganizations but moved from the person directly and purely. To the hungry and naked one gave food and clothing; to be in solidarity with the poor one became poor.

Personal action could also take institutional forms, but only if the personalist element was dominant and dynamic. Maurin used the works of mercy as an example: They could and should be practiced in the home but also in houses of hospitality. The use of personalist means in institutions thus precipitated an extension of the person into the social dynamics of the community. The introduction of pure means in an institutional framework was to be the peculiar contribution of Catholic sociology.[30]

Essential to Catholic activity was the harmony of hierarchy and laity working together, and Maurin's perception of a dynamic Church was encompassed in his understanding of this harmony. But that which was clear to Maurin after years of reflection was unclear to those who were just now becoming interested in the dynamism of the Church's message. In fact, it was the split between the clergy and the laity in the present that undermined the unity and efficacy of Church activity.

To Maurin, both the clergy and the laity were to blame. The laity had told the clergy to mind their own business, particularly in economic and political matters, and to retreat to an ever-diminishing sphere of doctrine and morals. By assenting to this retreat, the clergy had divorced themselves from the people, neglecting to acquaint themselves with and be among the masses. Because they were separated from the people, the clergy had lost touch with the social order and failed to provide a sociology that was grounded in theology, one that would join faith and social reform. This discouraged Maurin, for it meant that the clergy was not capable of or interested in a technique of leadership and thus would be unable to provide leadership for Catholic Action. Because of this failure of leadership people were leaving the Church and becoming interested in Marxism and fascism.[31]

This criticism of the clergy was made public in June 1934 in an essay Maurin published in the *Catholic Worker* titled "For Catholic Action." The tone of the essay, with its criticism of the clergy, was unusual for its time and evoked an immediate response from readers of the *Worker,* much of it critical. Some found Maurin to have overstated the case and suggested that perhaps the blame lay with a laity no longer attending to the matters of faith. To that Maurin reiterated the clergy's failure to provide a sociology linked with theology; their approach to social questions was either that of charity or that of books. This was not to say that the clergy could not be looked to for leadership. Maurin, however, was pessimistic as to whether such leadership would be forthcoming consistently. If it was to come, he felt that it would be generated by priests and scholars becoming workers, at least in their approach to social questions.

Maurin's public discussion of the clergy's faults raised many challenges, so the editors of the *Worker* replied in support of his view. For the four or five priests who were active, there were hundreds who paid no attention to the social teachings of the Church. It was the editors' view that most priests admitted this and that many appreciated Maurin's criticisms as a way of raising important questions.[32] This discussion of Catholic Action was broadened by Maurin's continuing dialogue with readers of the *Worker,* in response to questions raised about contemporary events.

A Catholic political party, for example, was proffered as a remedy for the extremes of Right and Left that resulted in fascism or communism. Maurin disagreed in a series of published replies that appeared in the *Worker* throughout the summer of 1934. The Holy Father, Maurin suggested, asked Catholics to reconstruct the social order not through Catholic political action but through Catholic *social* action, which Maurin had previously defined as the teaching of Christian doctrine, the daily practice of the works of mercy, and the founding of new Catholic institutions. The difference between political action and social action was subtle but important, for political action was wholly oriented toward the temporal order whereas Catholic social action was not interested in the temporal order as such but in the spiritual involved in the temporal. The difference, though, was more than orientation. Political action, built from above, could mobilize society in a variety of ways to reach political goals. Catholic social action, built from below, had only one goal, to serve God and, in serving God, to serve neighbor. Maurin pointed out further that Catholic political parties had vanished in Italy and Germany, and that communism could not be stopped by Catholic political parties. Fascism, whether Catholic or Protestant, could not stop communism either.[33]

Despite such discussion, Catholic Action as a theoretical position waiting to be actualized remained vague. If the faith and the leadership existed, the question of institutionalization and longevity still concerned many. How did one build through sacrifice? What forms were these hopes to take? Earlier in the year Maurin and Michael Gunn, organizer of the Catholic Labor Guild in Brooklyn, considered the potential of the organization of Catholic labor guilds throughout the country. The discussion, carried in the *Worker*, served to clarify Maurin's view of the forms Catholic Action could legitimately take, particularly regarding the principles of organization.

The question of organization was foremost. "Most organizations exist," Maurin wrote, "not for the benefit of the organized, but for the benefit of the organizers." When the organizers tried to organize the unorganized they did not organize themselves. Rather than organization, personal responsibility was stressed: "If everybody organized himself, everybody would be organized." Just as organizations to organize the unorganized left both the organized and the unorganized in a state of disorganization, assessments within the guild to build houses of hospitality likewise defeated the purpose of hospitality itself. For Maurin, the only money worth getting was the money given for charity's sake. Parish hospices had to be built on Christian charity.[34]

In defense of Catholic organization, Michael Gunn presented a view of his own Catholic Labor Guild as a model of general organization. The impetus to the Catholic Labor Guild was genuine and motivated by faith. Its fundamental values were rooted in daily spiritual exercises at Mass and Communion. Trade knowledge and labor were freely shared, often with little or no remuneration. The guild found guidance in the papal encyclicals of the time, which called for the selfless service that marked Maurin's ministry. Further, the Labor Guild assisted members financially and also with labor but did not accept interest for either. Labor was capital's partner and co-equal, and profits were equally divided between capital and labor. Gunn concluded that the guild offered full economic security as well as the organization for leadership that would minimize the threat of dictatorship.

Maurin's reply to these ideas was characteristic of his gentle nature and confidence in the correctness of his position. Assuring Gunn that though he found some of his ideas contrary to his own, he did like Gunn personally, for his life evidenced the values of poverty and service that Maurin espoused. In Maurin's view, the credibility of the guild turned on its function, and this was determined by whether the guild functioned as an institution that fostered the welfare of the masses or as a corporation to foster the wealth of a certain group. To function as an institution was to give to those in need, either giving freely as Christ had advised or lending without interest. If the Labor Guild did not lend money at interest, Maurin expressed the hope that it would not borrow money at interest either. If the guild stood for profit sharing, Maurin hoped that the members would also stand for loss sharing.

By functioning in this way, Maurin thought that the Guild would encourage the development of a Catholic aristocracy, which he thought essential to the development of a Christian democracy. However, this democracy was not to be based on class lines but on the assumption of leadership capabilities. To pay double wages to managers was to divide manager and worker into classes and move toward a corporation. Because "knowledge obliges," managers should receive what they need and no more. Maurin ended with an expression of his desire that the Labor Guild and the farming commune work together. The Labor Guild would help those it could help and the farming commune would help all those the guild could not.[35]

While Maurin could affirm the need for Catholic guilds and other organizations that maintained the "technique of institutions," he nevertheless followed his own vision of personal responsibility and self-organization. As Maurin's agitation gained a wider audience, this inevitably raised a series of difficult questions. Maurin constantly spoke about the teachings of the Church, particularly the papal encyclicals, but was his thought in line with teachings such as *The Conditions of the Working Class* and *Forty Years After?* The answer is complex. Maurin used a variety of techniques to pose questions, and one of these was to use encyclicals and ideas that he felt did not go far enough in the final analysis. Later, when he stated his own position, there could be much confusion.

Maurin's evolving message indicated his disappointment with the failure of certain papal encyclicals, such as *Forty Years After*, which were more organizational in their approach and did not uphold the ideal of personal responsibility voiced by the encyclicals on Saint Francis. It was as though "a sad and weary father said to his children who warred continually on one another: you will not follow the ideal so I will present to you another program—organization." During meetings at the Catholic Worker School, when speakers would affirm papal support for the New Deal, Maurin would rise and say, "The great danger of the present day is fascism and the tendency of all organization is to lead to fascism." Many of the visitors to the Worker and Dorothy Day herself found Maurin's analysis difficult to understand and accept. But Dorothy, sensing the importance Maurin placed on the subject, reaffirmed that the

Worker movement would continue to cling to the ideal as held up in the gospel and in the encyclicals on Saint Francis.[36]

The use by Maurin of the encyclicals on Francis was not tactical, for the influence of Francis of Assisi in Maurin's life had become considerable. The "clarification" Maurin experienced in the 1920s, which saw him change from a stable, fairly affluent French teacher in Chicago to that of an itinerant teacher and handyman in upstate New York, coincided with a worldwide revival of interest in the life of Francis and his own reading of Johannes Jørgensen's *Saint Francis of Assisi*, G. K. Chesterton's *St. Francis of Assisi*, and a series of papal encyclicals on Francis beginning with Leo XIII's encyclical *St. Francis and the Third Order*.[37]

Maurin not only read these works, he reflected on them. In one of his essays, Maurin used Jørgensen's understanding of Francis as a pilgrim, a life that Maurin had now adopted.

> According to Johannes Jørgensen
> a Danish convert living in Assisi
> St. Francis desired
> that men should give up
> superfluous possessions.
> St. Francis desired
> that men should work with their hands.
> St. Francis desired
> that men should offer their services
> as a gift.
> St. Francis desired
> that men should ask other people for help
> when work failed them.
> St. Francis desired
> that men should go through life
> giving thanks to God for His gifts.[38]

That Maurin emulated Francis's way of life is beyond doubt. By 1934, he had given up everything—home, status, financial security, and personal life. When he traveled around the country to spread his word, he came as a poor man and depended on others for hospitality. As much as anything, Maurin's adoption of Franciscan poverty was designed to free him to preach the Gospel and stand as a witness to a culture that prized affluence. His emphasis on faith and contemplation as the foundation for rebuilding the Church in a time of crisis was basically Franciscan, as was his emphasis on obedience to the Church, a theme he found crucial to Francis's ability to maintain his radicalism while avoiding sectarianism. Above all, Maurin's personalism, his patience with those afflicted, and a sense of joy compared favorably to, and received instruction from, the life of Francis. What he felt Francis "desired" of others, Maurin tried to live: He gave away superfluous goods, worked with his hands, offered his services as a gift, and went through life giving thanks to God.[39]

However, Maurin thought Francis to be more than a personal model. With the papal encyclicals on Francis, Maurin asserted that the mobilization of the Third Order could contribute significantly to the reconstruction of the social realm. The revitalization of Franciscan piety would occasion a rebirth of the dynamic lay faith for which Francis had hoped, and which through the centuries of Church life had been diluted. To this end, Maurin insisted that the evangelical counsel of the Gospels was for everybody and that the new society would be built on Franciscan qualities of creed, systematic unselfishness, and gentle personalism.[40]

As a modern follower of Francis, Maurin was profoundly at odds with the times in which he lived. While his desire for a new social order was prophetic, the central place of poverty in this new order proved a stumbling block for many. It was one thing to talk about Christians of the first century and the monasteries sacrificing for their faith and community in the practice of poverty, but it was quite another to bring the community face to face with the call to be poor in the present. Should poverty be pursued in a time of worldwide depression? Did not the first Christians, the Irish monks, and Francis himself sacrifice so as to make sacrifice unnecessary for future generations? Was not the taking on of poverty placing undue emphasis on suffering?

Though the questions were many, the answers in Maurin's

view had become clear. One became poor because Christ had given everything, even his life, to serve humankind. In his preaching Christ had spoken of the difficulty of the rich entering the Kingdom, and in his pilgrimage had made the poor his own. To become poor was to follow Christ and thus embody the message of salvation he had preached. This embodiment of the message of salvation was a witness to others of the importance of the spiritual, bidding them to follow. The personal and voluntary adoption of a life of poverty was a witness to the community as well and posed the prophetic question of the community's orientation: to the material or the spiritual. By adopting poverty the community could embody the message of salvation.

For Maurin, personal and community poverty was the road to the spirit and to freedom. If there was suffering within freedom, Christ had suffered, too. The person was free in giving up superfluous goods because life was ordered to its proper end: prayer and service, not sensuality and egoism. And the community was free because it was no longer consumed with the material. Instead of pursuing profit through competition, the community could now fulfill its primary function of encouraging cooperation and nurturing the spirituality of the person.

The freedom and the spirit that came in voluntary poverty was the most radical orientation possible and, when implemented in centuries past, caused significant, sometimes violent attempts to restructure social reality. Like others who had sought to emulate the saint from Assisi, Maurin saw Francis's poverty as eschatological. For to Maurin, Francis's vision of life, when embodied in the person *and* the community, broke through the constraints of history and institutional forms, radically questioning the lethargy and "givenness" of personal and social life. Francis thus represented the transformation that Maurin sought: a return by the person and the community to a total dependence on God. For Maurin, this included freeing the Church and the Franciscan orders themselves from the bureaucratization that had diluted the radical demands of Christ. With those who would later make Francis humanist and nature lover, Maurin would have no part. Through Francis, Maurin wanted to move to the beginning and the end: the following of Christ.[41]

Taking of Francis as a model, however, signaled more than personal and social commitment, for in following Francis Maurin found his place within the Catholic tradition. This had not been easy, as Maurin had moved from a peasant upbringing to Paris, Canada, and the United States. Surely his experiences had been diverse, from teaching as a Christian Brother, to participating in the social activism of *Sillon*, to wandering the breadth of America in search of work. At the age of fifty-seven and after much struggle and reflection, Maurin had finally found his way.

CHAPTER FOUR

Toward Harlem
and Holiness
1934

In May 1934 the *Catholic Worker* celebrated its first anniversary, and there was much to be thankful for. The circulation of the paper had increased from 2,500 to 35,000, and the appeals for support of the paper and the house of hospitality were generously answered. The movement had grown in numbers, too, with most of the recruits attracted and indoctrinated by Maurin himself.

One of the new recruits was Stanley Vishnewski, then seventeen years old. His own story of finding the Worker movement was representative of many who were to come over the years and illustrates Maurin's influence in the growth of the movement. Attracted to the personality of Christ and looking for the means of spreading Christ's kingdom on earth, Vishnewski stumbled on the little group who called themselves Catholic Workers, though it was not by mistake that he ended up there. In his unpublished personal history Vishnewski related his own problem of finding work in the social apostolate.

> In the year of 1934 there seemed to be no lay apostolic groups working in the United States to advance the Kingdom of God upon earth. The only place open for a young man who wanted to do something for God and His Church appeared to be in the formal religious orders. The laity were looked upon as second class citizens whose main function was to fall upon their knees and open their purses.

PETER MAURIN

There were those who claimed that the Counsels of Perfection were only for religious. The laity were to content themselves with obeying the Ten Commandments.[1]

Vishnewski began praying for a work that would absorb his life and his love. When he came across a copy of the *Catholic Worker* he decided to visit the editorial office.

A few days after reading the paper, Vishnewski visited the *Worker* office on Fifteenth Street and described the setting that had now become Maurin's home.

The flat was sparsely furnished. The front room, facing the street, which I took to be the editorial office was a long room, but rather narrow in width. The furniture consisted of several chairs, a broken down rolltop desk, which was supported upright by two books. On top of the desk was an upright typewriter.... Next to it was a large book case full of books. There was also a metal topped kitchen table which was used by Frank O'Donnell, the circulation manager, as a desk. The entire mailing list of the paper was kept in a small wooden file cabinet.... In the corner of the room by the window was a huge packing box filled with clothing which was reserved for the needy—anyone could (without any questions being asked) come in from off the street and help himself. Everyone was trusted to take what he needed. The heat was furnished by a pot-belly stove which stood in the center of the room. There was a dark and small middle room between the office and kitchen. On one side were shelves filled with back copies of *Commonweal, America, The Sign, Blackfriars.* The other side of the room was piled high with suitcases, which homeless people had left to be taken care of while they looked for a place to stay. An iron cot took up the last inch of available space. The kitchen itself was small and was dominated by a round table. It made me think of King Arthur and his Knights.... The table could seat about eight comfortably—though when extra guests were present a few wooden leaves had to be added to stretch the table.[2]

An hour after Vishnewski entered the office, Maurin came in and they talked. Vishnewski soon fell captive to Maurin's troubadour method of reciting his essays and to his knowledge, which Vishnewski thought inexhaustible. In the course of listening, Vishnewski discovered that Maurin had a program for Catholic social action based on the encyclicals of the Church and that he was for tradition, not for revolution. Maurin would tell Vishnewski that in the Catholic Worker movement the aim would be to have the voluntary poverty of Saint Francis, the charity of Saint Vincent de Paul, the intellectual approach of Saint Dominic, and the manual labor of Saint Benedict. As much as the ideas, Vishnewski recalled Maurin's person.

> Peter had a habit of rocking back and forth in his chair and occasionally he would lean over and tap you on your knee in order to emphasize a point. His face even then, I remember, had a sort of nobility about it and it was lined with wrinkles but somehow one never noticed Peter's appearance after he began to speak. He had the knack of making one deeply interested in his message.[3]

Soon Vishnewski was accompanying Maurin to Union Square and Columbus Circle to engage communists in discussion. The pace was grueling but, as Vishnewski remembers it, exciting. He and Maurin would arrive in Union Square at six o'clock in the evening and engage in discussion until six the next morning. With six hours of sleep they would awaken and hurry to noon Mass at St. Andrew's Church near Manhattan's City Hall. After Mass they would lunch at cheap restaurants on the Bowery, where the menus were written in soap on the glass windows.

Vishnewski represented one way of finding the Worker movement. But more often people who had lost everything in the depression would wander around Union Square and Columbus Circle, become attracted to Maurin's talks and be invited to the Worker office for hospitality. Dan Orr was one such person. He had been a truck driver and a policeman who one day came to the Worker wanting nothing more than to soak his tired feet. That night at supper Maurin indoctrinated him on the dignity of poverty and read to him some of Father Vincent McNabb's *Nazareth or Social Chaos*. Soon Orr began selling the *Catholic Worker* on the streets of New York City.

Edward Breen was another recruit. Breen had been a newspaperman with a long list of credits to his name, among them being the former Sunday editor of the *Washington Post* and a press agent for President Coolidge. When another paper he had edited ceased publication he found himself without work. Breen's life was a mixture of sadness and profanity. His wife had died from tuberculosis as had his only child, and his voice would lower and break whenever he mentioned them. At other times, though, his voice would grow loud as he shouted racist expletives like "kikes," "dagos," "niggers," at people with whom he became angry. At times he waved his cane around his head, threatening to disable his opponents. But, like many others who came to the Worker movement Breen became an important part of the community and after a few months found a permanent place there. His job was to sit by the door and greet visitors.[4]

Even with this growth of their community the life of the Worker was still precarious. "God seems to intend us to depend solely on Him," the editorial column of the anniversary issue stated:

> We must live this lesson of dependence on Him that we preach in these pages. Economic security, something every reader and we ourselves would like to have, is not for us. But what security did the Blessed Virgin herself have as she fled in the night with the Baby in her arms to go into a strange country?[5]

The Worker's apostolate was equally tenuous. It was hard to quote the Gospel to men and women with empty stomachs, to preach "holy poverty" to those who were destitute, lacking the basic necessities of life not only for themselves but for their loved ones as well. The best that could be done was to assure readers that most who were writing for the paper had known dislocation too, had experienced hunger and cold, had slept in city lodging houses, in doorways, and in public parks, and had walked the city searching for work. Maurin, of course, was no exception.

Though the conditions were difficult, the Catholic Worker

apostolate was spreading beyond its own doors, and the newspaper was being recognized in other journals. *Orate Fratres* (later *Worship*) greeted the appearance of the *Worker* with satisfaction. "It appears a veritable godsend in our time of social disintegration and unrest." What impressed *Orate Fratres* particularly was the Christian foundation and the "thoroughly Catholic spirit that breathes through its pages." John Toomey, a Jesuit, wrote an enthusiastic article for *America*, noting that "the response to the paper has been simply tremendous. It seemed from the beginning to voice the unspoken thoughts of millions." Priests were ordering bundles of the newspaper for their churches and sisters were buying it for their schools. Farmers, miners, and textile workers were reading it. A priest in Hamburg, Germany, was distributing one hundred copies every month to American and English seamen he found on the Hamburg docks, and lay people in Australia were distributing it there. Toomey concluded that month by month the *Catholic Worker*, the "little Catholic monitor, is pouring Encyclical fire into red and reactionary merrimacs."[6]

Maurin himself was the subject of several articles. J. G. Brunini, writing in *Commonweal*, termed Maurin an apostle to the radicals. Brunini described his technique, which had now become familiar to those gathered in Union Square:

> Maurin does not employ a soap-box. From audiences he questions socialist or communist speakers and defends the position of the Catholic Church. Or he will initiate a discussion with one or two or three bystanders, gradually collect a crowd and address it although ostensibly talking only to his original listeners.[7]

The presence of communists at Maurin's talks had the value of making Catholic workers who otherwise would remain silent "decidedly articulate." In Brunini's view, this had the effect of strengthening their faith. He concluded that Maurin had initiated discussion for the clarification of thought that had been advocated by the recent popes.[8]

John LaFarge wrote affectionately though critically of Maurin in an article in *America*. Describing him as an elderly, peaceful man who wanted to apply ethics to the complicated question of wealth, LaFarge thought Maurin's language perfectly familiar five centuries ago, but confusing in the present: "It is as when you cannot ring a bell without getting a jarring resonance from a cracked window pane." LaFarge continued:

> In a conference, let us say, on social surveys, or some other finely graduated thesis, when discussion begins to languish, Peter stands up—not very high and conspiciously inconspicuous—and without further preludes tells the audience that "in the first centuries of Christianity the poor were fed, clothed and sheltered at a personal sacrifice."[9]

Maurin would continue:

> And because the poor
> were fed, clothed, and sheltered
> at a personal sacrifice,
> the pagans used to say
> about the Christians
> "See how they love each other."
> In our own day
> the poor are no longer
> fed, clothed, and sheltered
> at a personal sacrifice
> but at the expense
> of the taxpayers.
> And because the poor
> are no longer
> fed, clothed and sheltered
> the pagans say about the Christians
> "See how they pass the buck."[10]

It was particularly important to LaFarge that Maurin lived the life of simplicity and poverty that he preached. Yet, while recognizing Maurin's voice as prophetic, LaFarge also raised piercing questions. What would Maurin do if he had a wife and six children to support? Could the ideals he proposed be seriously entertained as a general solution to the world's economic malaise? Maurin would reply that these ideals were something to strive toward, and, furthermore, that the movement toward ideals could be accomplished only through discussion and clarification. Instead of providing blueprints, Maurin hoped to raise questions that could not be denied. If his vocation was to live the single life, his farming communes, especially, were designed for families as well. Though these questions remained problematic to LaFarge, they did not lessen his respect for Maurin and he promised to pray for the success of Maurin's still theoretical farming communes.[11]

There were others who were praying for the success of Maurin's venture. In November 1934, Jacques Maritain, the French Thomistic philosopher, visited the Worker and had several discussions with Maurin. On Maritain's leaving he wrote to Maurin:

> I wish I could have said all that was in my heart—never was I more vexed by inability to speak fluent English. It seemed as if I had found again in the Catholic Worker a little of the atmosphere of Peguy's office in the Rue de la Sorbonne. And so much good will, such courage, such generosity! It is thus, with meagre means and great love, that the future for which we long is prepared.[12]

Maurin's essays were also beginning to reach a wider audience. In January and July 1934, *Catholic Mind* reprinted several of his essays dealing with the role of Catholic Action and the call for social reconstruction. At the same time Maurin's essays began to appear in pamphlet form printed by the Catholic Worker Press. These were penny and two-penny pamphlets ranging from two to thirty pages in length and included essays on hospitality, usury, and the works of mercy. The latter pamphlets were briefly noted in *Commonweal*.[13]

Another avenue for Maurin's essays was the development of the *Daily Catholic Worker*, an extension of the monthly publication. Instead of a printed newspaper eight to twelve pages in length, this was a mimeographed sheet distributed daily at the rate of a thousand a day. The typical daily carried provocative statements on the news of the day and concluded with one of Maurin's essays, though usually in shortened form. This experiment for agitation proposed by Maurin himself lasted little more than a month. Yet despite the brevity of its duration the paper gained attention, with *America* citing it as the first Catholic daily in New York City and important for those interested in the laborer's plight and the claims of social justice.[14]

Maurin spread his message through his own travels as well as through the written word. Two priests, who had been following Maurin's essays in the *Worker* for some time and felt that he was the one to challenge the apathy they had found, extended an invitation from Assumption College in Ontario, Canada. The college would finance his journey, and because they knew the nature of the Worker movement, they would send his expenses ahead of time. Meetings would be held through open forums and study groups in local parishes. The priests emphasized that Maurin's lack of university training should not deter him from coming, for rather than degrees, the students needed someone to inspire them, to show them that faith was something living and that it could have "a marvelous effect on human life."[15]

As was the custom, the invitation was accepted for Maurin by Dorothy Day. In accepting, she mused that the priests had invited the right man, for as she was writing he was sitting in the front office "haranguing" some visitors and getting them "charged up for action." Dorothy wrote that Maurin would be glad to come for a week, but added a plea that he be provided a return ticket to New York, as this would prevent his using the money to go somewhere else, perhaps to visit his friends in Montana or some equally distant place.[16]

Similar instructions from Dorothy were given to another group that invited Maurin to upstate New York. Dorothy asked that Maurin be back early in the week, for a demonstration was scheduled and speaking engagements had been planned. A week later Dorothy wrote to a correspondent, "God forbid that the railroads give Peter a pass. He'd be wandering all over the country and we'd never keep up with him. We need him here."[17]

Dorothy had a point in making these conditions. Maurin would disappear for weeks at a time, only occasionally writing to tell her his itinerary or when he would return. He was now fifty-seven years old, his method of travel was by bus, and his good fortune was determined by the hospitality of others. Naturally, Dorothy worried.

Maurin's search for clarity rarely stopped at the horizons of the intellect, and his meetings, discussions, and travels hardly quenched his desire to be for and among the people. Instead, it was his radical sense of mission that saw the unity of thought and action. The willingness to embody his thoughts and convictions led Maurin into a variety of strange encounters and one of them, in the spring of 1934, was Harlem.

By 1934 the fate of blacks in America had become central in Maurin's thought. This was not a sudden consideration. Maurin had roomed with a black in his years of wandering and had been in contact with blacks through Father LaFarge, and the *Catholic Worker* had run many articles decrying racial discrimination. Moreover, the depression hit blacks particularly hard, and the Scottsboro Case, in which nine Alabama blacks had been convicted of rape, was then prominent. All of this may have enhanced Maurin's sense of the urgency of the racial issue. In the final analysis, though, it was Maurin's sense of personal responsibility that sent him to Harlem.

In its May 1934 issue the *Catholic Worker* addressed the question of relations between Catholics and blacks. The *Worker* noted that a battle had begun among divergent groups for the loyalty of this dispossessed people. The communists had various clubs and organizations in Harlem making a "play for the Negro," and the editorial reported that Trotskyites had gone so far as to predict that the black masses would form the vanguard of the revolutionary movement in America. That blacks were oppressed was not to be questioned but to Maurin what was at issue was whether blacks would be educated to class warfare or "apprised of the Church's stand in the realm of social justice." To apprise blacks of the Church's stand meant a personal presence in the black community. If a store could be found cheaply enough, Maurin and some of his friends who were presently sleeping in the Worker office would volunteer to establish a residence there and conduct discussions and distribute literature to those who wandered in.[18]

In the same issue of the paper Maurin first pronounced his

concern for blacks, in a rephrasing of the bishops' annual statement of 1934. As stated by the bishops:

> There is a very grave and subtle danger of infection from Communism. Special efforts are being made to win Negroes who are the victims of injustice. The Communists have as their objective a world war on God and the complete destruction of all supernatural and even natural religion.

Maurin rephrased the statement:

> The Negroes are beginning to find out
> that wage-slavery
> is no improvement
> on chattel-slavery.
> The Communists say
> that Christianity is a failure
> for the very good reason
> that Christianity has not been tried.[19]

With the donation of a store by Paul Daley, a Catholic attorney, Maurin and Herman Hergenhan left the Fifteenth Street house and made their home in Harlem, at 2070 Seventh Avenue just below 124th Street. Both the *Daily Catholic Worker* of May 22 and the June issue of the *Catholic Worker* announced the opening of the Harlem storefront with enthusiasm. It was to be not only a place where interested blacks could ask questions concerning Catholicism, but also a center for maintaining an active program of meetings emphasizing social justice and racial equality. Since the communist idea of a godless state had been concealed from the blacks, it was the object of the Harlem branch to show blacks that the Church had a definite social program and that there was interest in all workers, black and white.[20]

On May 21, Maurin and Hergenhan moved into the storefront. Hergenhan, a Protestant, was an old friend of Maurin's from Union Square and had just completed a series on municipal lodging houses for the *Worker*, drawing on his own personal experience. As a result of the depression, he had lost his job as a carpenter, and, when his savings were exhausted, lost his home too. A life of "comparative affluence" had ended and soon Hergenhan was sharing a park bench with others of the same situation. Finally, with no funds and nowhere to sleep, he was housed at the municipal shelter for indigents. Thus Hergenhan had firsthand experience of the commercial charity against which Maurin had spoken, and felt that he had "joined the ranks of social outcasts." This experience radicalized him, and when he heard Maurin in Union Square Hergenhan made his way to the Worker. Maurin had lectured him on a variety of subjects and now the two were friends. Though a Protestant, Hergenhan's ideal, like Maurin's, was the Thomistic common good. They would work together, Hergenhan giving speeches and Maurin distributing literature and leading conversations on street corners.[21]

The Harlem branch they opened was anything but formal. A laundry sign hung over the door and the floor, though clean, was bare of any covering, requiring a day to hammer down nails that had held down former layers of linoleum. There was no furniture until, some days after the opening, a neighbor donated a bed and covers. Soon to follow were donations of tables and chairs, pots and pans, a tool chest, and some boards for shelves. In the beginning there was no money to turn on the electricity or even for candles, and Maurin received evening guests in the dark. One such guest was Father LaFarge, who remembered his visit because all he could see in the dark was Maurin's forefinger motioning in the air as he was making his points. Often, because of lack of funds, Maurin begged for food or money. Later a statue of a black Madonna that had hung in the Fifteenth Street house was delivered and hung in the Harlem storefront.[22]

By the middle of September it was reported to the donor of the storefront that Maurin and Hergenhan were living comfortably, holding meetings, and carrying on an educational campaign that had gained credibility through their sharing the people's poverty. It was also reported that books, magazines, and blackboards lined the wall with Catholic teaching, and that Maurin was already taking in men off the street and sheltering them.[23]

PETER MAURIN

By October the Harlem program was in full swing. In the evenings there were discussions, with the leadership alternating among laity, priests, and black speakers. On Friday night Hergenhan held forth while Maurin spoke on Saturday night. The afternoons featured art, catechetics, and story hours. Emile LaVallee, a professor of French, had joined the group in Harlem, and both he and Maurin conducted French classes as well.[24]

Maurin discoursed on a variety of subjects in Harlem, but on the "Negro issue" his point was singular. If anthropologists divided the world into four kinds of people with blacks being a distinct group, they added at the same time that there was nothing in science to prove one race superior to another race. Theologians made the same point: that Christ died for the redemption of all races. Blacks were created by the same God and enjoyed the same beatific vision. For Maurin the conclusion was obvious: All races were included in the Mystical Body of Christ. If there was a "Negro problem" in America the solution was not the emulation of values whites had held out for blacks in slavery or capitalism but the development of black culture. The way for blacks to solve the Negro problem was to behave the way Saint Augustine, a black man, wanted everyone to behave, as believers looking after each other. For Maurin, it was the power of example.

> The white people
> are in a mess
> and the Negro people
> will be in a mess as long as they try
> to keep up
> with white people.
> When the Negro people
> will have found the way
> out of their mess
> by evolving a technique
> in harmony
> with the ideology
> of Saint Augustine
> the white people will no longer
> look down

on Negro people
but will look up
to Negro people.
When the white people
will look up
to the Negro people
they will imitate
the Negro people.
The power of Negro people
over white people
will then be the power of example.[25]

By the middle of October, initial enthusiasm was blunted
by the difficulties of being white and Catholic in black and
Protestant surroundings. Writing to a correspondent, Dorothy
Day expressed dismay. "I wish you would drop in to see Peter
when you have time. It is pretty hard sledding up there. There
is great opposition to the work and it is hard to get along." The
next day Dorothy wrote to another correspondent in the same
vein. "His school is not going well at all and only a few people
show up. The place will just have to continue as an information
and literature center and for the meeting of friendly groups."
Dorothy noted, however, one successful aspect of the venture,
for the arts and crafts classes conducted by Ade Bethune and
Julia Porcelli were well received and thriving.[26]

Maurin's venture in Harlem could not be faulted for lack
of imagination. To spread his message one night, Maurin went
on as an amateur performer at the famous Apollo Theatre. He
was announced as a comedian, and when he began reciting his
essays, catcalls filled the theater. Maurin was escorted off the
stage. Later he recalled that he really "got the hook that night."
Maurin also conceived the idea of having "poster walks" in
which a group of young men, each carrying a sign with an idea
from one of his essays, would walk through the streets of Harlem. They would walk in a straight line, becoming something
of a moving billboard. A group of students agreed to participate in the march, but the marchers were abruptly dispersed
by a barrage of insults and garbage hurled at them by members
of the Harlem community. This was not the only such incident

of violence for the Workers; one night Maurin was accosted by two thugs in Harlem who jumped him and gave him a severe beating. When he showed up at the office, his face was a mass of bruises.[27]

Violence of yet greater magnitude was witnessed by people at the Harlem storefront. In March 1935, a riot broke out in Harlem spurred by the depression and rumors that a black child had been beaten to death by the police. Hergenhan, in an article that appeared in the April 1935 issue of the *Catholic Worker*, described the situation as "indescribably tense," bordering on "terrible furor." One night, as the evening classes at the Harlem center drew to a close, the shattering of glass was heard. The door was locked and all sat in the rear of the house. At midnight the disturbance reached a climax as window after window in neighborhood houses fell to the sidewalk until their own block was invaded and groups of angry blacks surrounded the storefront. Just as the destruction of the storefront seemed imminent, a man in the crowd voiced the opinion that these white people should be left alone, that they were "all right." The center was spared and the next day friends of the Worker, black and white, came to make sure all was safe.[28]

"God's miracle," as it was described by Hergenhan, strengthened Maurin's determination but did not enhance the blacks' acceptance of the Workers' positions. Six months later, despite distribution of leaflets proclaiming the Church's stand against war and fascism of any kind, there was still a marked reluctance to receive the paper. On several occasions the tabloid was torn up. Finally the Harlem center closed when the owner, a member of the National Guard, found out about the developing pacifist stand in the Worker movement and asked Maurin and his cohorts to leave.[29]

Even before the riot in Harlem, many doubted the purpose of a Catholic Worker branch there. Some were skeptical of the usefulness of the work, while others thought it wasted effort. Hergenhan illustrated the prevalent attitudes.

> Teaching a few small children a few small things, they reasoned, would not remove the stench of race discrimination; handing out a few free copies of *The Catholic Worker* would

not, they held, convince an oppressed people of the efficacy
of Catholic Worker philosophy.[30]

These understandings could not be easily dismissed. A
willingness to go to the poorest, the least, was often an invitation to failure, and Maurin's Harlem work did precisely that—
it failed. Yet Maurin judged success and failure in ways quite
different from the usual, for his dialectic of success and failure,
characteristic of his life and thought, rested ultimately on an
interpretation of history and the person. Maurin's interpreta-
tions were only suggested in his earlier essays, but became ex-
plicit in the summer of 1935 when he published in the *Catholic
Worker* a written digest of Nicholas Berdyaev's essay "The
Bourgeois Mind" and an original essay "In the Light of History."

Nicholas Berdyaev (1874–1948), a Russian philosopher exiled for his opposition to the Russian Revolution, saw the central historical problem of his age as the ascendancy of the
bourgeois spirit. For Berdyaev, the word "bourgeois" designated not a social, economic, or ethical condition but rather a
spiritual state and a direction of the soul. In essence, the bourgeois spirit was a pursuit of the material aspects of life and an
endless search for the expedient and the useful. The bourgeois
was an "idolater" of this world.

Though the bourgeois spirit had always existed in culture,
it had reached its apex in the nineteenth century. Berdyaev saw
then that its concupiscence was no longer restricted by super-
natural belief as it was in the past, no longer kept in bounds by
the "sacred symbolism of a nobler traditional culture." The
knight and the monk, the philosopher and the poet, had been
superseded by the bourgeoisie interested in business and trade.
The center of life, the spiritual, had been exiled to the periphery.

The triumph of the bourgeois spirit led Berdyaev to de-
clare that history was a story of failure. Nor was the present an
improvement on the past, for periods of high cultural development were succeeded by cultures that had qualitatively deteriorated. Berdyaev lamented that the will to power and affluence
had triumphed over the will to holiness and genius. The high-

est spiritual achievements belonged to the past, and no longer could historical progress be claimed.[31]

Maurin accepted Berdyaev's definition of the bourgeois spirit as a spiritual and ontological condition and his proposition that history was not inherently progressive. In Maurin's own essay "In the Light of History," he traced the development of the bourgeois spirit as a pattern of decline spanning the previous 800 years. This decline began with the demise of the medieval system, which Maurin placed around the year 1400. For Maurin, medieval society had been a model of economic good sense because trade and commerce were governed by Canon Law in recognition of the primacy of the community and the spiritual. The economy itself revolved around the meeting of needs rather than wants and desires, thus defining a functional rather than an acquisitive society. Because the producer dealt directly with the consumer, there was a sense of personal responsibility and integrity for the craftsman and the farmer. This was exemplified in the doctrine adhered to by the guilds, the doctrine of the common good.

Around 1400, the middleman appeared and helped usher in mercantile capitalism. The middleman offered to buy the goods of the guild and market them, and guild interest turned from the common good to money. Because markets were geographically separated from the place of production, consumers rarely met producers. With this lack of personal proximity, producers ceased to think in terms of service to the community and became interested solely in profit. By 1600, under the impetus of Calvinism, a further separation of economy and community control occurred with the legalization of moneylending at interest. In 200 years the use of currency had shifted precipitously from a means of exchange in a functional society to a means of making money in an acquisitive society. Maurin noted the interesting transposition that had occurred: People lent money on time and started to think of time as money.

With the discovery of steam power, factory capitalism made its appearance around the year 1700. Those who had been interested in expanding markets for goods now began building factories, ostensibly to produce goods that would take drudgery out of the home. To produce goods that had once been produced in the home, members of the guilds left their shops for the factory. The manufacturer, though, was less interested in easing labor than in producing profit. It was cheaper to employ women and children in the factories than it was to employ men. Thus, women and children were employed outside the home and unemployment among men increased—a situation Maurin felt was detrimental to the family.

By 1800, most Western countries subscribed to the argument of Adam Smith that competition was essential to trade, and within this competition only the fit would survive. To survive in an industrial world one had to look for markets to garner new materials and distribute goods and to protect these markets, a need arose to dominate other countries. Of necessity, industrial nations adopted imperialist foreign policies. This external competition soon required the internal security of each nation's interests, and in this lay the origins of monopoly capitalism. Monopoly capitalism welcomed trusts and high tariffs to protect industries, unions to protect "proletarianized" workers, and federal intervention to protect consumers and conserve raw materials. Maurin thought that this combination of external competition for markets and internal protection of industry led to the increasing power of the state and the hostility of England and Germany in World War I.

The war itself was another stage in the decline of history, for it ushered in the era of finance capitalism. In Maurin's view, the war was fought primarily for commercial reasons, but to mobilize each nation the fighting had to be idealized, prompting the call to a war for democracy. The war for democracy, however, brought not democracy but its antithesis: Marxism in Russia, fascism in Italy, and nazism in Germany. This failure of the war, though, did not dampen the enthusiasm of the "progressive" mentality. Installment buying fueled a belief that, with the end of the war, a new era had dawned: an era of mass distribution of goods and increasing, perhaps never-ending prosperity.

The year 1929 brought what Maurin considered the last watershed, the world depression that ushered in state capitalism. Economics had failed of themselves and now economic activities, credit, and employment were to be supervised by state bureaucrats. Six years after the depression had begun, despite protestations that the economic system was fundamentally sound and that prosperity was around the corner, economic recovery was still remote. In Maurin's view, the last 800 years had led only toward chaos and destruction.[32]

There were underlying themes that highlighted the stages of decline and that were central to Maurin's view of history. These stages were illustrated by economic movements, primarily the rise of capitalism, with the implicit view that the failure of capitalism eventually led to totalitarian regimes on the left and the right. The rise of the middleman and the legalization of moneylending at interest, for example, demonstrated changes in values to a new emphasis on profit and consumption. Finally, this heightened interest in profit and consumption indicated a shift in orientation from the spirit to the object, from the mystical to the worldly, disputing—even ending—the efficacy of traditional religions. For Maurin, as for Berdyaev, the 800 years of decline had been more than the rise of a new economic system and organizational propensities. It had been the triumph of a secular world guided by self-interest over a religious world once guided by tradition.

The end of cultural and religious tradition involved in the decline Maurin detailed could not be taken lightly, and Maurin spoke often on this subject as the summer of 1935 drew to a close. For thousands of years tradition had provided a sense of continuity and rootedness to persons, to communities, and even to civilizations. To deny tradition was in a profound way to be separated from the past, the spirit, and the struggles and conclusions found within both. In Maurin's view, the soul was intimately bound up in the spiritual, but the modern world allowed fewer avenues for the person to recognize and follow that which could not be stilled: the yearning of the soul for eternity. The end of tradition was not simply secularization, but economic, military, and political systems freed from the guidance of the spirit and thus from protection afforded the person by the canopy of eternity. Maurin had become convinced that it was tradition that held worldly systems at bay and molded them to serve rather than to oppress the person.

The disappearance of tradition ultimately led to the devaluation of the person.[33]

The voices of the spirit, however, would not go away. In the constant battle with bourgeois mentality, the voices of tradition subverted the secular view of every age. Maurin constantly counterposed the present with tradition. If the moneylenders were the first people on "Uncle Sam's payroll," there were no moneylenders on the payroll in Palestine and Ireland because the prophets of Israel and the Fathers of the Church forbade moneylending at interest. If nobody today dared to drive the moneylenders out of the Temple, Christ had. If there were no ethics in modern society, there had been ethics in society when Canon Law was the law of the land. And if one laughed at the thought that the Irish had once reconstructed Europe after the barbarian invasions with guest houses and farming communes, Maurin replied that the accomplishments of the Irish missionaries after the fall of the Roman empire could be "done today during and after the fall of modern empires." In essence, then, tradition was a sacred history, a collection of people and cultures that had witnessed to ideals that were ever constant and had never been superseded. The aim was not to move beyond this history but to recover the holy ways that had come to fruition in times past.[34]

How could these holy ways be recovered? Only by the individual, in freedom and conscience, appropriating tradition and living within it. In this way the person inherited and communicated the truth and wisdom of times past and crystallized both in the finding of personal vocation. The binding of tradition and vocation was possible because in a world of contingency and materiality the person, as a spiritual being, rose above the necessity of time and matter. In Maurin's view this was done through interior development and responsible activity and by affirming a hierarchy of values, though they might run counter to contemporary values.

The choosing of vocation, as Maurin's own life so aptly demonstrated, was more than a path toward a career. It represented the sum of the person's freedom and thus the freedom of the person was bound up in affirming truth. Maurin accepted

Emmanuel Mounier's definition of vocation "as a metaphysical response to a metaphysical call, an adventure in the eternal order of things, set before each man in the solitude of his own choice and his own responsibility."[35]

But to be a person was to live in community, and the choosing of vocation always had as one of its objects love of neighbor. The question of the person living in community was complex and occupied much of Maurin's time and energy in the ensuing years. Maurin later referred to a personalist living in community as a "communitarian personalist," balancing the integrity of conscience and the needs of the community. The task of each person was to reach a spiritual destiny with the aim of Christian heroism and holiness in a community of persons.[36]

CHAPTER FIVE

Cult, Culture, and Cultivation 1935–1937

From his study of the past and his analysis of the person and community, Maurin became convinced that the foundations of personal and community life were to be found in the coincidence of three elements: religion, learning, and the land. For these Maurin formulated his own terminology: cult, culture, and cultivation. In November 1935 Maurin published an essay in the *Catholic Worker* entitled "Back to Christ—Back to the Land!" that outlined the evils of the present that were hindering community. At the same time he pointed to this new synthesis of cult, culture, and cultivation, linking the return to a religious life with a return to life on the land.

The essay began with an analysis of the breakdown of community in the present. Maurin charged industrialism and mechanized labor with undermining the person's sense of self-worth. This was true for a variety of reasons. Industrialization forced urbanization and inaugurated a system of impersonal arrangements that destroyed rural cultures and values. Furthermore, the fruit of industrialism, mechanized labor, deprived the worker of creative labor. Because the factory hand had no responsibility for production and factory operations required little thought and originality, the worker had been reduced to a "subhuman" condition of intellectual responsibility. In the largest sense, industrialism and mechanized labor had deprived the masses of the two bases of community: family and meaningful work.

Maurin contrasted "machine civilization" with "handicraft civilization" through the example of a Chinese immigrant. At first the Chinese was dazzled by the material progress of America and even had hopes of transplanting American ways to China. After returning home he thought differently. His was a handicraft civilization and the differences with America were irreconcilable. There was a smallness and integrity about the products China produced. If industrialism came to China, the people would change and cultural traditions would be destroyed. To Maurin, this was more than just a case of the clash between Western and Eastern civilizations. It portrayed a transformation occurring within all countries that demonstrated the triumph of industrialism over traditional cultures and thus over civilization itself.

Maurin defined handicraft civilization as a society where agriculture was practiced by most people and crafts by others. The archetype of such a society was the rural village, for it was in the village structure that those involved with agriculture and crafts maintained personal responsibility for their labor. Because workers produced for the needs of the community and used tools rather than machines, there was an integrity about their work. If mechanized labor had divorced the notion of work and utility from the notion of art and the beautiful, farming and craft labor held the potential to once again bring them into unity.

The difference between rural and urban attitudes was as significant to Maurin as the difference between handicraft and industrial civilizations. Because life on the land encouraged cooperation and a functional economy, the desire for wages and profits would diminish, even fade away, in a rural society. Unemployment would end and the transitory, contractual quality of industrial relationships in work and marriage would find a new stability. Living on the land instead of in the artificial world of the city, the person's philosophy of life would be organic rather than mechanistic, familial rather than individualistic. Children would be welcome and the aged respected. The community would, as ideally sought, be oriented around the good of one another.[1]

This revival of responsibility for and integrity of labor in an agrarian, handicraft civilization not only brought about a sense of self-worth and dignity but also instilled in the laborer a love of learning. It did so because of the personal interdependence of the community members, and because each bore responsibility for providing an important service to the community. Rather than being a "cog in the wheel of mass production" and thus passive, the person was thrown back on his own initiative, thriving on the mastering of situations within and for a community enterprise. In Maurin's view, personal initiative and the necessity of mastering situations called for the intelligence of the person and desire to participate in the development of beauty, thus encouraging the development of culture.

Cult was at the center of this synthesis of cultivation and culture because, as the person's being was imbued with transcendence, its fulfillment required participation in divine life. Religion served as the foundation of life on the land and culture because cult gave unity to personal and community thought and aspiration. Life could be ordered and fulfilled only when it was oriented around its center, the spiritual life.[2]

By 1935, then, Maurin's vision of a future society had come into view. The escape from industrialism and secularism was not in capitalism or state socialism, but in a return to a society where agriculture was practiced by most of the people in a faith context. Quoting Andrew Nelson Lytle, Maurin wrote, "It is in fact impossible for any culture to be sound and healthy without a proper respect for the soil." In relation to the spiritual life Maurin then quoted Ralph Adams Cram: "And there is no sound and righteous and enduring community where all its members are not substantially of one mind in matters of the spirit—that is to say, of religion."[3]

As was his style, Maurin's intellectual agitation had its counterpart in activity, and in March 1935, a new column made its appearance in the *Catholic Worker* addressing itself to the possibility of starting a farming commune. The initial piece announced that, come spring, the Worker movement was going to make an effort in another direction and attempt to open a combination farm and school. Though this new venture was less than the agronomic university or farming commune Maurin envisioned, it was a step toward fulfilling his program.

By June the Workers' hope had become a reality, for a Catholic farming commune on Staten Island was in the making. Maurin's friend H. Hergenhan wrote with enthusiasm about the commune's prospects, reflecting that, to those who were addicted to a boss and a pay envelope, it would seem a ludicrous idea to return to the land. But to reach a higher cultural level, the individual had to be "lifted out of the mire of social economist degradation," and to ensure personal independence one had to be rid of industrialism. To humanize "large hordes of slum-dwellers" was to restore them to their natural heritage—creative work on the land. It was in the renascence of a rural economy that the foundation for a more rational and just social order was to be laid.[4]

The commune was small, with about an acre of land, and the editors decided to describe the experiment as a garden, rather than farm, commune. The house, though, was large, with twelve rooms. On the first floor, in addition to the kitchen, there were three rooms in which meetings were to be held. A porch ran around the house. To the rear was a stretch of open land and on one side were thick woods.[5]

As time progressed it became evident that there were problems on the garden commune, problems that were to plague future Worker agrarian experiments as well. The most obvious root of discord was the conflict between the philosophies of the workers and the scholars, which Maurin had hoped could be brought into unity. The workers wanted only to work with their hands and appreciated concrete results; though the scholars wanted these visible results, they also had a sense of the intellectual dimension of the farm experiment. The workers could not quite appreciate the expenditures of effort called for in organizing discussion groups and planning programs. Nor could they appreciate that it was donations from the visitors who enjoyed these conferences that financed the manual work and the commune itself. Yet the workers' perception was only a part of the problem, for the scholars, too, were to blame. As Dorothy Day recalled:

> Too often, although motivated by the desire to avoid pass-
> ing judgment on others, he would withdraw into silence.
> Sometimes it was the scholar's inability to communicate ex-
> cept to his peers that prevented the workers from following
> him. It was only natural for them to want a genial compan-
> ion, rather than a silent, aloof, or a glibly articulate one.[6]

Maurin was the sole exception to this worker-scholar split, combining manual labor and reflection and refusing to dis-criminate in his associations between the intellectual and the worker.[7]

The failure of workers and scholars to labor together in harmony was a disappointment to Maurin, as his hope was that both would lend their particular skills to the community. There was something more, though, for Maurin hoped that by the scholars' participating in manual labor they would gain a concrete basis for theory. Through intellectuals' affirming the dignity of labor, workers would not only understand their own dignity but would respect thought and want to participate in the world of ideas. The participation of intellectuals in manual labor and workers in the world of ideas would create integrated persons.

Though the problems remained, the search for a larger farm was begun and this search was itself an occasion for a clarification of Maurin's ideas. In the February 1936 issue of the *Catholic Worker*, Cyril Echele, a friend and disciple of Maur-in's, reflected on the philosophical and practical basis of a farm-ing commune. Man was a person before God, thus the commune movement would be personalist with a stress on in-dividual freedom and initiative. Because the person was also a social being, the cooperation and goodwill of others were essen-tial and the commune therefore would be personal *and* commu-nal. This community spirit would be based on the doctrine of the Mystical Body of Christ; it would be kept alive through in-doctrination, common labor, and liturgical prayer.

Those who came to the commune to learn farming skills

would be approved regardless of their status, social class, or skills and would be given food, clothing, and shelter; they were required to bring only their goodwill. The people, though, had to be full-time participants in what Echele called the "re-establishment of a Catholic culture," a goal that could be accomplished only by work on the land and the practice of Catholic life. Echele was adamant on this point. Those who came just to rest or study would be considered "externs" and not members of the commune; those unwilling to make "the whole sacrifice, to go the whole way" were wasting their own time and that of the commune.

Diversified farming would be practiced as much as the soil and climate allowed, and conservation of the land would be practiced by rotation of crops and manuring. In regard to machinery, any tool or machine that was "the extension of the hand of man" would be used, though horse power and mule power would also be utilized. Cultivation of the land was to be enhanced by the implementation of cult and culture. Like Maurin, Echele thought that the three processes would be mutually supportive and carried out simultaneously. "Whether we be out in the field sowing or in the woods cutting fuel our every action is a prayer. If we work individually our act is an individual prayer; if we work together our action is a social prayer." Culture could also be developed during work, especially when work was halted to engage in conversations about issues of import.[8]

By April 1936 the search ended with the finding of a farm. Located two and one-half miles out of Easton, Pennsylvania, and seventy-one miles from New York City, the farm lay atop a mountain where fields stretched out for twenty-eight acres, overlooking a beautiful valley. The land was covered with peach, apple, and cherry trees. The outbuildings were badly in need of repair and the orchards, too, needed work. Eight acres of the land was woodland. The price of the farm was just over a thousand dollars, paid through recent donations.[9]

Many questions arose concerning this new venture. To some, the farming commune seemed to be an escape from the frustration of city life and the tragedy of urban poverty, and they wondered whether some Workers were not retiring to lead peaceful lives in the country. In reply, the editors of the *Worker* noted that the work in the city continued both in the house of hospitality and the lectures of the Catholic Worker School, but that from the beginning these had been proposed as halfway measures leading ultimately to a rebirth of life on the land. The time to begin this movement back to the land was now. As for ease, the farming commune provided anything but leisure. It was the Workers' hope to establish an "essentially Catholic community, *living* a truly Catholic culture." To have a community of interests and a common culture it was essential to form a community physically as well. This was possible on an extensive scale only on a farm, for a farm community would free people from an alien social system and allow the free development of their own. The question of whether there would be room for anyone but farmers on the commune was answered in the affirmative. Ideally, the farming commune would be better called a village commune and would include many crafts and occupations.[10]

A month earlier, Dorothy Weston Coddington, one of the first Workers and one highly influenced by Maurin, wrote of the need to combine cult and cultivation in the journal *Liturgy and Sociology*. The farming commune, she asserted, provided spiritual isolation from the influence of a pagan society and culture as well as the ability to be economically self-sufficient. Moreover, it provided what was necessary from the viewpoint of Catholic philosophy: the reintegration of the material and the spiritual in the body and the soul of the person, through work and religious belief. For Coddington, as for Maurin, the return to farming communes would give people labor meaningful in working out the person's salvation. Coddington wrote, "It is the necessity of bridging the hiatus between our Catholic sense of values and the work we must do for a living that makes us insist on the basically agricultural community as the way of life from which a Catholic society will grow." This goal could not be reached except in a nonindustrial setting.[11]

As the farming commune moved forward in theory and fact, news arrived that a paperbound edition of Maurin's essays was to be published by Sheed and Ward. The book became available in June 1936 and bore the title *Easy Essays*. It was 112 pages in length and was divided into sections, each prefaced with an illustration by Ade Bethune who, following Maurin's suggestion, depicted Christ and the saints as workers. All but one of the essays had already been published in the *Catholic Worker*, though editing added a certain clarity to them.[12]

Publication of the book gave Dorothy Day a chance to write about Maurin and his ideas, and in doing this she clarified somewhat the nature of the man who was behind the movement. She indicated that Maurin wrote under protest for he did not consider himself a writer but a speaker; his essays were written only because people did not always listen when he spoke. To those who refused to listen, Maurin had habitually written his point and mailed it to them. His essays had been written in unusual circumstances: in a barn by the light of a lantern in Woodstock; at a boys' camp on Mount Tremper; in coffeehouses along the Bowery; on benches in Union Square. It was nothing for Maurin to stop on a picket line and jot down phrases in his notebook. Often he would stir from meditation in church to pen a line or two.

At one time universities were built around such a man, Dorothy reflected. In the Middle Ages the teacher *was* the university, and like Maurin, these teachers had indulged in easy conversations about matters of significance. At that time, the teacher rather than fine buildings had attracted students. Dorothy lamented that now the buildings overshadowed the teacher, and the "loans of the bankers smother[ed] thought and expression."

There was nothing that bound or constricted Maurin, and to Dorothy he was the most detached of men. If it was true that when he moved from place to place he took a suitcase, it was a suitcase full of books. If he had an extra shirt he gave it away, and the change in his pocket belonged to the poor. Since the beginning of the Worker they had tried to give him a room of his own, but he would never take it. There was always someone in need, and if none came along, Maurin would find someone in need to share his quarters. He also had an uncritical attitude regarding other people. He never judged or condemned a person. In Dorothy's view, Maurin's enemies were principalities and powers, not flesh and blood.

Maurin, of course, had his faults. He would come in from the West with a handful of money given for subscriptions to the *Worker* but would have misplaced the list of subscribers. One time he had an important interview with a professor from the University of Chicago but had neglected to get his name, thus rendering the interview useless for publication.[13]

There would also be misunderstandings. Maurin could be vague, and inevitably Dorothy bore the responsibility of straightening out difficulties that ensued. One such case, in the fall of 1935, involved the publication of a fortnightly review entitled the *Communitarian*. Maurin had encouraged two young enthusisasts, Richard Deverall and Thomas Barry, to begin the journal, which had been Maurin's idea. The mission of the journal was to emphasize the communal aspects of Christianity, in effect explaining in depth the foundations of the Catholic Worker program. Physically it would have an appearance similar to other Catholic periodicals such as *America* and *Commonweal*. Its content, however, would differ and be comprised of Catholic social thought written in a way that the common person could grasp. Works of contemporary Christian writers would be extracted and these would include works of Maritain, Mounier, and Berdyaev as well as Maurin's essays.

Apparently with Maurin's blessings, Barry and Deverall had stationery printed and began soliciting contributions for the journal-to-be. On the masthead he was listed as an editor, but Maurin was upset that he was so listed and instructed Dorothy to write to Deverall in an attempt to have his name struck from the editorial board. "Peter, strangely enough, did not understand just what you were going to do," Dorothy wrote. Though he had long advocated a quarterly magazine that would deal in detail with the communitarian ideal, Maurin understood that both Deverall and Barry were to first prepare for such an endeavor through reading and experience. Dorothy made it clear that Maurin wished his name removed from the masthead and that they should postpone their review until they had the requisite knowledge of the communitarian ideal itself. The problem, of course, was that checks and subscriptions were already coming in and that Father Furfey, among others, had promised an article for the review. In the end, the review

101

came out with a different format, entitled the *Christian Front*, and minus Maurin as editor.[14]

Maurin could also get angry. This anger was exemplified in the argument over the relative importance of the works of mercy and indoctrination, a question raised by a group called the Campions. The Campions grew up within the Worker movement and hoped to make it more "efficient" in transforming the social order by emphasizing indoctrination over the works of mercy. Thus they hoped to divert the money that had been contributed to the Worker for the feeding of the poor to the uses of propaganda and printing. By the fall of 1936, there was no longer a possibility of clarification. Name-calling occurred: Some referred to the men and women from the streets as "derelicts," "rotten lumber," and "deadwood." This incensed Maurin. One evening while eating supper he turned to Dorothy Day and said: "Come, let us go. Let us leave the paper and the house to them." To Maurin the issue was important as a principle. The way to reach people was by agitation *and* by the works of mercy carried on at a personal sacrifice. To preach the principles of a new society one had to embody these principles. One did not abandon the helpless for "efficiency."[15]

The beginning of the farm and the publication of his book made Maurin more anxious to spread his program. Thus, the May 1936 issue of the *Catholic Worker* announced a series of round-table discussions to be chaired by Maurin from May 26 to June 30 in cities around the country, specifically Milwaukee, Chicago, Cincinnati, and Pittsburgh.

Maurin's visit to Chicago was especially fruitful. As with other cities on the itinerary, he had appeared there before accompanied by Dorothy Day. Their previous appearance in Chicago had not only increased the circulation of the *Worker*, but had also helped awaken students to the evils of racial discrimination. Starting on June 9, at the St. Ignatius Library on West Roosevelt Road, Maurin chaired discussions on Catholic Action, capitalism, fascism and communism, race relations, farming communes, and Catholic education. Among the participants in the series was Arthur Falls, a black doctor and a friend of the Worker movement. As usual, Maurin's accommodations were unusual. He spent the first several nights on a bench in the Greyhound bus terminal, and the last night in a room reserved for bishops and other visiting dignitaries at St. Ignatius Church.[16]

After Maurin's visit Dr. Falls wrote to the *Worker* declaring the sessions a success, and terming the discussions the most instructive and interesting heard among Chicago Catholics for a long time. With the stimulating series of round-table discussions completed, a Chicago unit of the Catholic Worker was formed and was ready to appeal to Chicago friends for a house of hospitality. Temporary quarters had already been established at the residence of a woman who for many years had been engaged in the works of mercy on her own initiative.[17]

While Maurin was busy in Chicago, previous visits he had made to Boston were coming to fruition in the founding of a hospice and food center. Like the New York and Chicago houses, the Boston house was located in a poor neighborhood, as Maurin suggested. Those who came for relief would find it in their own environment, thus preventing embarrassment. Round-table discussions were already under way, and once a farming commune could be found Maurin's program would be completed. A farming commune was being planned and would finally materialize in Upton, Massachusetts.[18]

A Catholic Worker center had just been opened in St. Louis, and a variety of activities had been carried out. CIO circulars had been distributed at steel plants, lectures offered by a Catholic labor organizer about the necessity of labor organizing among Catholics had been heard, and a young woman had used their quarters for a catechism class for black children. Though the St. Louis group lacked the proper facilities for serving food, they had fed some men who had wandered in off the street. As with all the houses of hospitality, the survival of the St. Louis center depended on charity, and the donation of fifteen dollars by a group of nuns and three dollars from a parish priest, which went for rent and unpaid bills, was duly noted. Above all, the group was concentrating on Maurin's program calling for "clarification of thought" leading ultimately to a "unity of mind." The group would feed and clothe the poor as much as was possible with the available resources. With Maurin, the St. Louis group knew that there could be no Christian revolution without a theory of revolution, and that the theory of Christian revolution was intimately bound up in the practice of religion. Only then would they be ready for Catholic Action.[19]

Maurin's thought had also reached overseas with the founding of the English Catholic Worker movement. The English group, like the New York Workers, was faced with the forces of capitalist and communist materialsm. Thus the English Workers promised to oppose materialism with the "spiritual sword of Christ." The English Catholic Workers believed that the means used must be different from those used by other revolutionaries. The means would be the forces of spirituality; those who joined their work would reemphasize the liturgy and bring about a change through "personal sanctification." Like those active in the New York Worker movement, their ambition was to be "papal rather than left-wing." Accordingly, they would expound on the pope's encyclicals concerning social questions and urge a reconstruction of the social order in a Christlike spirit. They would start a newspaper and the English *Catholic Worker* would reprint Maurin's essays, because in their "simple and intensely spiritual tone" they had a "worldwide and not only an American appeal."[20]

As the Catholic Worker movement grew in size and influence, the question inevitably arose as to what kind of alliances a Catholic movement could form, and on what base those alliances could rest. Maurin had affirmed the need for a working relationship with others of various faiths and had said so in print as early as July 1934. Referring to Hergenhan, his Protestant friend and co-agitator in Harlem, Maurin challenged Catholics to live up to his example. Hergenhan believed that the Thomistic doctrine of the common good was common to "humanists who are human, to Jews who are orthodox, to Protestants who are Christian, and to Catholics who are Catholic." To Maurin, the "Common Good movement," rather than being a movement that divided, was one that united.[21]

The November 1936 issue of the *Catholic Worker* carried an essay of Maurin's entitled "The Pluralist State," in which he addressed the topic of commonalities and alliances at some length. Maurin wrote that the affirmation of human personality was the common belief of the differing traditions, and that this common belief in the person provided the framework for cooperative ventures. The ideal of cooperation would be to build a pluralist society. This pluralist society would be based on the cultural tradition of the Western world, which affirmed the integrity and spiritual dimension of the person, a tradition Maurin felt had been betrayed by utilitarian, laissez-faire, and totalitarian ideologies. What would a pluralist society be like? It would be a place where people of varying traditions lived up to their highest calling and to do this the pluralist state would not pass laws and create bureaucracy in an attempt to solve social problems, but would remove all laws that hindered social movements based on personal responsibility. In such a society, Maurin envisioned the diminution of the state's responsibility to a coordination of relief in times of natural disaster and major crisis. In effect, the state would be replaced by the predominance of the cooperative, guild, agrarian, and communitarian movements.[22]

Cooperation with non-Catholic groups was a controversial idea and in a letter published in the February 1937 issue of the *Catholic Worker*, Thomas Barry reacted strongly against the idea of working for a pluralist society. Barry thought there was already too much "baptism" of the cooperative movement. The cooperative movement was distinctively bourgeois in character and too much in the line of enlightened selfishness to become a spiritual entity. The curse of Christian social movements had been compromise. "We are too damned eager to embrace all the potential brothers of Christ before they are ready for it," Barry wrote. "We cannot go to God with soiled souls." Reassuring people for doing less than they ought to was good propaganda, perhaps, but bad Christianity; to love people enough to love their sins and heresies was to have something wrong with our love. Such a course was to have "fallen into humanism and fallen out of love of God." Barry suggested that Catholics would do better to leave the cooperatives to Protestants and unbelievers.[23]

Bryan Degnan replied to Barry and defended Maurin's position. Though Barry had given sound warnings about the dangers of superficial cooperation, Degnan thought Barry wrong when he completely rejected the benefits possible through co-operation. To Degnan, embracing part of another position was not embracing the entire position. When Maurin quoted the opinions of Dr. Kagawa, a Protestant, on cooperatives, he was not endorsing his spirituality. Instead, Degnan noted, "We are humbly thankful to [him] for pointing out to us a sign that there is a simple Christian truth which many of us capitalistic Catholics have betrayed. Why not cooperate with cooperation at least to the extent of gentle personalism?" Degnan inquired. At the same time the Catholics' own brand of spirituality would remain distinct. "If they see the shining splendor of our own Catholic cooperatives, will not that light be for the Common Good?"[24]

As disturbing to Maurin as the lack of cooperation in moving toward a new social order was modern education's inability to provide a basis for the responsible independence of the person. In an essay entitled "Back to Newmanism," published in the December 1936 issue of the *Catholic Worker*, Maurin quoted Cardinal Newman:

> If the intellect is a good thing then its cultivation is an excellent thing. It must be cultivated not only as a good thing but as a useful thing. . . . It must be used by the owner for the good of himself and for the good of the world.[25]

This was the ideal, although Maurin found present forms of education wanting. He used a personal example. When he first arrived in New York City, Maurin had asked professors to give him concepts that would enable the common man to create a "universal economy." Inevitably the reply was, "That is not my subject." For Maurin, this answer lacked integrity, for it was not enough merely to master subjects. Education was designed to enable people to govern themselves and to actively participate in the shaping of community life. If modern education turned out a variety of specialists, they knew more and more about less and less. This resulted in the inability of the person to develop self-government and to interact critically with the surrounding social order. Such an educational system produced students able to enter the status quo, but not those who could create "order out of chaos." Maurin thought the consequences of import in the modern trend toward increasing apathy and passivity in the face of unparalleled crisis.[26]

Maurin's critique was followed by a proposal for the creation of "outdoor universities," which would leave behind classroom education for "dynamic" education. For knowledge to be dynamic, it had to "rub shoulders with the man on the street." To do this, though, it had to be presented in the people's vernacular. The outdoor university would provide a forum where the restatement of scholarly ideas could take place. Students would come from all walks of life—the unemployed, laborers, business people, and college graduates—to seek clarification in a combination of theory and physical labor. Physical labor would provide a shared, concrete context out of which theory would evolve. Professors of an outdoor university would be different from their academic counterparts, for instead of looking for endowments they would look for manual labor. Professors would not dictate to students but would teach by example. Instead of mastering subjects, students would be taught to master situations. Professors of an outdoor university would not teach their students how to make lucrative deals, but would teach them how to realize worthy ideals. Education, then, would become a way of preparing people for their vocation.[27]

As a professor of an outdoor university himself, Maurin attempted to take his message to professors and students of academic universities, and proposed the founding of houses of hospitality near secular universities. These would function as "centers of light," where college students would combine theory with service to the poor and thus develop a holistic view of reality.

Harvard University provided a starting place for the implementation of Maurin's idea. Etienne Gilson, the Catholic medievalist, was lecturing there in the fall of 1936, and Maurin felt that Harvard was ripe for his own agitation. No halls were available and Monsignor Hickey, the pastor of Saint Paul's Church, the closest church to Harvard, thought his mission impossible, especially because of what he termed "Harvard indifferentism." Maurin, however, was not dismayed and decided to give his lectures on the Boston Common, hoping that some Harvard students would attend and carry back his message. The lectures on the common were a success, and one day the crowd stayed for over five hours as Maurin analyzed the need for a new approach to education.

After the lectures, he returned to the Boston house of hospitality, where discussion continued late into the night. On two occasions there Maurin traced the history of education in New England before an audience comprised of teachers, librarians, and students. Maurin pointed out that in its beginning, education at Harvard and Yale was centered on theology. However, with the secularization of learning the elective system of education had triumphed. This was producing a curriculum without focus or integration. What was needed was a revival of the tutorial system, which, in Maurin's view, would bring back a more profound culture.

Maurin also voiced displeasure with the idea of mass education. At times it appeared to be a method aimed at keeping children off the street, and since the emphasis was on social studies it resulted primarily in an accumulation of facts. Children were made "fact-foolish," and schools and universities "fact-factories." Maurin felt that to be truly educated, one had to be grounded in philosophy and religion. This gave the context for understanding and interpreting life. In contrast to unintegrated education was the ancient monastic system in which monks would have several children live with them, allowing a religious and philosophical education by showing them a life of dedication. Maurin proposed this system for the present.[28]

The role of the professor as a model of life and the transmitter of thought to the uninitiated could be applied as well to the "thinking journalist." Maurin reflected on the educational role of journalism in response to a request by the *Record*, the student paper of St. John's University, Collegeville, Minnesota, for an essay to commemorate their fiftieth anniversary in January 1937. He began with an example. To report that a man died leaving two million dollars was part of journalism but was not necessarily good journalism. Good journalism was to tell everybody that at the time of his death the man had two million dollars because he did not recognize the value of giving it to the poor during his lifetime. Like the professor, the journalist was not just to report a fact or a happening but to take personal responsibility for the event and place it in perspective, that is, to "give the news and the right comment on the news." Instead of offering a passive reflection on the culture, the journalist was to be instrumental in creating public opinion. By affecting public opinion, the thinking journalist became a "creative agent" in the making of news rather than simply being a recorder of modern history. The journalist would aim "to be a maker of that kind of history that is worth recording."[29]

Maurin did not limit the need to be creative agents to professors and journalists, for social workers, too, needed redirection. The primary problem with the training of social workers was that it taught them to adjust to the existing environment instead of learning how to change the environment. To become critics of the environment and free creative agents of a new environment, social workers first had to become aware of the workings of society. Houses of hospitality could provide the context in which the understanding of social forces could be learned so as to make social workers creative agents rather than adapters.[30]

Beyond the questions of education and journalism, the role of labor organizations was becoming urgent to Maurin and to the Worker movement itself. Surely labor issues were some of the most difficult issues the movement faced in the 1930s. From the beginning, the Worker had sided with the laborer even to the point of dedicating the paper to workers. The strikes the paper supported were numerous, such as the National Biscuit Company strike in March 1935 and the Borden Milk Company strike in January 1936. The support of unionization was complex, though, especially in light of the Worker's philosophical positions. The predominant forces in unionization were capitalist or communist; the former saw unionization as a goal for participation in the capitalist system while the latter viewed unionization as a way of mobilizing for class warfare. The Worker supported neither goal. If this was not complex enough, the support of strikes attracted the scorn of many Catholic and non-Catholic Americans who saw any pro-union activity as both pro-communist and anti-American.

PETER MAURIN

As was often the case in the history of the Catholic Worker movement, external events lent urgency and depth to the clarification of policy and principle. The Seamen's Strike in the spring of 1936 started as a spontaneous protest against the policies of both the shipowners and the International Seamen's Union. The strike appealed to the Worker movement because of the recognition that neither owner nor union was serving the laborers themselves. By the fall of 1936 the Workers were feeding thousands of seamen a day and housing hundreds.

The ambiguity of the Worker stance warranted clarification and in a front-page editorial in the July 1936 issue of the *Catholic Worker* Dorothy Day sought to provide this. Above all, Dorothy wanted to be honest, for the support of strikes was not primarily on the ground of wages or conditions of labor "but on the fundamental truth that men should be treated not as chattels, but as human beings," as "temples of the Holy Ghost." When laborers were asserting their rights to be treated as persons and to be considered partners in a common enterprise, they were fighting against the idea of labor as a commodity. This, Dorothy thought, should be supported. While the movement rejected both the capitalist and communist labor organizations, it would support the unions as "organizations of workers wherein they can be indoctrinated and taught to rebuild the social order." However, the support of unions was to be only a step in the movement back to the land.[31]

One reason for clarification of the Worker movement's stance on unionization and strikes was Maurin's negative position on both, and his constant refrain that "strikes don't strike me." The reason for this opposition was clear to him, although vague and sometimes controversial to others. To Maurin, the organization of societal forces inevitably led to confrontation and violence. But there was more to his position than fear of polarization. Once erected, organizational structures themselves would militate against the deep-seated change in the forms of work he felt essential to the well-being of the person. Instead of the organization of labor, Maurin was interested in developing what he called a philosophy of labor.

Maurin's philosophy of labor was much the same as that of

Eric Gill, the English craftsman and social philosopher. It rested on the idea that manual labor was essential to the continuance of life, and that it was intrinsically good for both the body and spirit. Physical labor was human labor, demanding intelligence, skill, and personal initiative. Modern society found manual labor degrading, but Maurin thought it ought to be sanctified, and he quoted Gill: "At every turn our object must be to sanctify rather than to exclude physical labor. To honor it rather than to degrade it, to discover how to make it pleasant rather than onerous, a source of pride rather than shame." Physical labor directed to the production of things needed for human life was honorable and, in a profound sense, holy.[32]

Maurin thought that industrialization and mechanization had been prime factors in the degradation of labor and therefore of the person. The worker was alienated not only from the means of production, as Marx had claimed, but from the process of production as well. Thus, reclamation of the person was intrinsically bound up with the reinstitution of labor outside of the industrial setting. Maurin's was a long-range program: He looked for ownership by the workers of the means of production, the abolition of the assembly line, decentralized factories, and the restoration of crafts and ownership of property. Any organization that did not in the long range look to the end of industrial society was not to be supported.[33]

Maurin's theories on industrialism and industrial organization were confronted directly with the formation of the Association of Catholic Trade Unionists (ACTU), an organization that began at a meeting around the kitchen table of the New York house of hospitality and had as one of its leaders a Catholic Worker named John Cort. In an article published in the March 1937 issue of the *Catholic Worker*, the hopes of the organization were spelled out: to create a militant, effective opposition to communist and anticommunist domination of American unions by being a positive force for social reconstruction on Catholic lines. The guidelines for the association fell into three categories: enrolling all Catholic trade unionists in the association; promoting unionization of unorganized Catholic workers; applying Catholic doctrine to the trade union movement. The beginnings of the union were a success and gained much of that success through the backing of the Catholic Worker.[34]

Maurin, however, remained in opposition, grounding his stance in his "philosophy of labor," which opposed industrialization. This position remained an issue over the years with those who thought it possible to "Christianize" the industrial process. John Cort was then and remained Maurin's most vocal opponent on the subject. Cort recalled:

> I did not accept the argument of Peter Maurin and others at the Catholic Worker that the solution to the industrial system was to flee the cities and go back to the land and to making things by hand. This seemed to me to be a lovely and romantic notion that would never appeal to more than a select few who rarely had the money or the hand-muscled skill and determination to make it work. In short, counterproductive and highly distracting. It was a debate that raged for years, at times even more violently than the battles over pacifism and anarchism.... Peter's gentle/rugged individualism could take the spiritual discipline of the Catholic Church but not the temporal discipline of a trade union. For Peter the whole scene was unnecessary and distracting. He abominated the machine age even more than he abominated organization. Better to pull the weeds out with your own hands than to compromise with the assembly line and industrialism.[35]

But to the surprise of both Maurin and his opponents, Maurin was "struck by a strike," the sit-down strike introduced in 1937 by the United Automobile Workers and used in March of the same year at the Woolworth and Grand Stores in New York City. Reflecting on this phenomenon, Maurin amended his position somewhat in an essay entitled "The Sit-Down Technique," which was published the following month in the *Catholic Worker*. The sit-down strike appealed to Maurin because it emphasized nonviolence and avoided the polarization that picket lines symbolized. In the sit-down strike no one struck anybody "either on the jaw or under the belt." As long as it was conducted on Gandhian lines, conforming to the doctrine of pure means, Maurin felt he could support it. According to Maurin, the sit-down strike was necessitated by the refusal of business to accept responsibility for depressions. The positive side of the sit-down strike was that it expressed the desire of the laborer to cooperate in the running of business and to achieve collective bargaining. Under the present system, collective bargaining and compulsory arbitration would at least assure the worker of the right to work.

Still, Maurin's support for organized labor remained qualified. Whether it was the American Federation of Labor or the Congress of Industrial Organizations, organized labor was far from certain of how to deal with the economy. Organized labor, organized capital, and organized politics were the products of the modern mind and, therefore, essentially secularist. Instead of condemning them, though, Maurin sought to use the organizations for his own purposes, and promptly proposed the association of Catholic employers to function alongside the associations of Catholic workers. In this way, employers and employees would be indoctrinated with the same principles. Maurin's hope was that these organizations might develop leaders who would "lead us in the making of a path from things as they are to the things as they should be"—that is, back to the village.[36]

In October 1937, Maurin was interviewed on a radio program, and the text of the session was transcribed and published in the November issue of the *Catholic Worker*. Questions had been submitted in advance and Maurin's answers had been prepared. The answers represented a summation of much of his philosophy as his words attained a greater clarity divorced from the essay format.

Maurin suggested that the first step toward the solution of the current economic malaise was to feed, clothe, and shelter the needy, and to instruct the ignorant "for Christ's sake." If the first step, in the words of the interviewer, was to spiritualize service to others by expressing the spiritual in the material, the question remained as to how to achieve this. Maurin replied that his idea was "to have people who choose to be voluntary poor live under the same roof and sit at the same table with the unvoluntary poor." This would set an example in the "spiritualization of human relations" that others could follow.

The job of the voluntary poor and their associates was to remind the owners of capital of their responsibilities, and to teach the worker that labor was a gift rather than a commodity to be sold. The responsibility of ownership was not found in acquiring more wealth since all wealth belonged to God. Rather, the owner was "God's trustee," and the profits of industry had to be used for the children of God. As Leon Harmel suggested, the profits of industry should be used for looking after the needy of the community. Industrial owners needed to act as aristocrats rather than plutocrats toward their workers and in the community in general. Maurin also defined the laborers' responsibilities in terms of the common good. The worker was to take pride in work well done and make things that were "fit to use rather than sell." Above all, the worker had to realize that labor was related to thought and that thought was not a commodity but a "spiritual faculty."

When the owner and the worker realized their responsibilities both could contribute to the formation of a functional society based on Christian charity. This functional society was one in which the members fostered the common good. It was a society where people were willing to give rather than get, a society made up of idealists rather than materialists. The practical way of achieving this society was through the personal initiative of those who had learned how to use their freedom, and who kept in mind that means had to harmonize with the ultimate ends pursued.

Where would people find the principles of social reconstruction? They would find them in the social teachings of the Catholic Church through the centuries. To the question of how one could bring about this change in the social order, Maurin cited six ways: daily practice of the works of mercy at a personal sacrifice; round-table discussions and study groups to clarify thought and activity; joint action of workers' and employers' associations to bring about collective bargaining; "impregnation" of these associations with Christian principles; development of farming communes for the unemployed; responsible participation in this program wherever and however one found the opportunity.

The final question was one Maurin delighted in answering and one that brought into focus his own philosophy. In answering the question that, in light of the conditions of the time, some thought Christianity had failed, Maurin returned to Chesterton, asserting that Christianity had not failed because it had not been tried.

> Christianity has not been tried because people thought that it was not practical and men have tried everything except Christianity. Everything that men have tried has failed, and to fail in everything that man tries is not considered practical by the so-called practical people. So the so-called practical people will begin to be practical when they start to practice the Christianity they profess to believe in.[37]

The Christianity Maurin professed to believe in, and thought so important to live, was being practiced by the movement he had founded. This had been confirmed earlier in the year by William R. O'Connor, a professor of Dogmatic Theology at St. Joseph's Seminary at Yonkers, New York, when he visited the Catholic Workers and published an article reflecting on his visit in the *Ecclesiastical Review* titled "Primitive Christianity in New York City."

To come to the Worker house of hospitality was a bewildering experience, O'Connor reflected, for once inside it was like stepping over twenty centuries and landing in the time of the apostles. For here was a group of people living as the early Christians of Jerusalem had lived, becoming poor themselves and living among the poor in fidelity to the Gospel. O'Connor confirmed what Maurin had hoped for: Catholic Workers were making an effort to live Christianity, not just talk about it.

What was their way of life? It was "startlingly similar" to life described in Acts 2 and 4, a life of sharing in common and being of one heart and mind in spiritual matters. There could be no question about the sincerity and genuineness of their Catholicity. They were all believers, attended daily Mass, and were devoted to liturgical prayers. "If you enter the little kitchen behind the office you may catch a young man reading a book of devotions or you may be engaged in a conversation on the Mystical Body," O'Connor wrote. Catholic Workers were not playing at these prayers and conversations, for those who faced the hard realities of life and did not know where their next meal was coming from could not afford the luxury of play. O'Connor felt that the results of this service and prayer were stunning. For those who came hungry in body and soul, both hungers were being satisfied.

That those at the Worker houses of hospitality held all things in common did not mean they were communistic in the present political sense of the term. Here, once again, O'Connor witnessed Maurin's theory in practice. Catholic Workers were not philanthropists in the Victorian sense of the term, stooping down to raise the workers and the poor to a higher plane. Neither were they communists in the Marxist sense, dragging all down to a common level. Rather, the Workers exemplified Apostolic communism, something midway between the other two views. The Worker movement transcended class distinctions and O'Connor thought this followed Romans 10:12 and Galatians 3:28, ending the distinction between Jew and Greek, slave and freeman, male and female, all becoming one in Christ. This absence of distinction made it difficult to tell who were guests and who were hosts. "There is a complete identification of themselves [Catholic Workers] with the ones they serve—they give up their beds and sleep on a couch or even on the floor when there is an overflow of guests." All of this was voluntary and done at a personal sacrifice. Those who served and those who were served were one.[38]

CHAPTER SIX

Personalist Democracy and the Land 1937–1939

Despite the controversy over cooperating with other movements and faiths, Maurin continued to work for the formation of a personalist and pluralist society. Toward this end, he spent much of the fall of 1937 organizing a series of monthly symposia on personalist democracy. These symposia took place at the Labor Temple on East Fourteenth Street, beginning in January 1938.

The meetings were skillfully organized and well attended. Maurin was listed as the coordinator of the meetings and, true to his intentions, the sponsors represented a wide spectrum of traditions: as Personalist-Humanist, Roger N. Baldwin of the American Civil Liberties Union; Personalist-Theist, Louis Finkelstein of the Jewish Theological Seminary; Personalist-Christian, A. J. Muste of the Labor Temple; Personalist-Catholic, Carlton Hayes of Columbia University. The purpose of the symposia was described as the "clarification of thought by free presentation and discussion of a subject of common concern." The speakers were to give full expression to their beliefs without "any intention to minimize or dilute in search for a common denominator."[1]

The January symposium began with remarks on the philosophy of personalism by Roger Baldwin. After reading the *Personalist Manifesto* by Emmanuel Mounier (suggested to Baldwin by Maurin), Baldwin explained that the manifesto was driving at a contemporary expression of an old and basic principle of life: "That all institutions find their ultimate justification only in the degree that they contribute to our personal growth and development of the individual, to the highest of which he is capable." It condemned, too, all instruments of force and violence through which a class society was held together. "I long ago came to the conclusion that as long as the state as an institution exists, as long as this instrument of violence continues, you could not have real liberty." For Baldwin, this was true in both a working class state and a capitalist state.[2]

Eugene Kohn delivered the second talk, addressing the role of religious principles in social reconstruction. Kohn characterized the problem of the age as domination by the machine. Though invented to serve human needs, the machine had created a situation of dependency in which the servant had become the master. Such had happened not only with physical machines but social machinery as well. Maurin agreed with Kohn's statement:

> To such an extent does mechanism dominate our whole culture that we are often disposed to think of all nature as a vast machine, an organization of power and nothing more. Ideals seem illusory, consciousness itself a mere recording of the pressure of blind forces. In the cosmos we hear the whir of the engine rather than the music of the spheres.[3]

The function of religion in reconstructing society was to release modern culture from the hypnotic spell of the machine so that society would again be recognized as a community of souls rather than forces. Only personalist democracy could fulfill this desire. By extending the principles of democracy from the political to the economic sphere, personalist democracy would represent an advance in harmony with the sacredness of human personality.[4]

A. J. Muste's remarks were equally interesting. Personalist democracy, differing from communist and fascist societal organization, could never conceive of the social problem as being primarily one of political arrangements. The fundamental question had less to do with external factors than with the essential nature of the human being. If a person was a being of moral dignity and worth, able to function in a free community, then democracy was possible. The perception of human beings as responsible and capable of great dignity raised the question of God in a positive way. The vision of a free and just social order could be encouraged by the revival of religious experience.[5]

Maurin could agree with all of these thoughts, for they confirmed his essential belief that those who lived out their own traditions came to similar conclusions about the possibility of a human social order. In this spirit, Maurin ended the first symposium with a recitation of some of his own essays, which moved the discussion from philosophy to the possibility of personalist activity.

"They" and "We"

1. People say:

    "They don't do this,
    They don't do that,
    They ought to do this,
    They ought to do that."

2. Always "They,"
        never "I."

3. It starts with "I."

4. One "I"
        and one "I"
        make two "I's."

5. And two "I's"
        make "We"
        for "We"
        is the plural of "I."

6. "We" is a community
        and "They" is a crowd.

119

7. "They" is a mob
   "They" is a gang
   and "They" are gangsters.

WHAT MAKES MAN HUMAN

1. To give and not to take
   that is what makes man human

2. To serve and not to rule,
   that is what makes man human

3. To help and not to crush
   that is what makes man human

4. To nourish and not to devour
   that is what makes man human

5. And if need be
   to die and not to live
   that is what makes man human

6. Ideals and not deals
   that is what makes man human

7. Creed and not greed
   that is what makes man human[6]

Maurin's interest in the democratic ideal was neither new nor was it fleeting, as his following symposia amply demonstrated. With the rise of totalitarian regimes in the mid-thirties, he frequently discussed the possibilities of democracy as the decade's close saw the question become increasingly urgent. His understanding of democracy was influenced by many thinkers, for example, Don Luigi Sturzo, the Italian priest and politician, and Jacques Maritain. Maurin took particular note of an article written by Sturzo entitled "The Spirit of Democracy" and Maritain's book *The Twilight of Civilization.* Sturzo's essay began with the definition of the spirit of democracy as the freedom achieved in social life with reference to authority, an authority in which the entire people shared according to their own capacities and in cooperation for the common good. Thus democracy in Sturzo's view was more than the assertion of rights by individuals in pursuit of individual gain. It was a political and social system, organized on a basis of freedom for the common good. The point was neither to destroy nor to defend present democracies, but to work toward change from the present as it was. One could uphold present democracies only where they actually were democratic, thus affirming what was fundamental and permanent while hoping to regain the true foundations of democracy. What were the true foundations of democracy? Here Maurin quoted Maritain:

> If the western democracies are not to be swept away, if a night centuries long is not to descend on our civilization, then the Democracies must discover the principle of life in all of its purity, which is justice, justice and charity, whose origin is in God.[7]

With the assertion that belief in God provided the foundations and possibilities of democracy, Maurin distanced himself from liberal democratic theory, which began with the individual and the relative nature of values outside the individual, and from Marxist and fascist theory, for with all their differences, both subordinated the person to the process of history made absolute. Maurin's understanding of democracy was different because he viewed the person as absolute not in and of himself but in relation to a tradition that oriented one toward transcendence. The democratic aspect of life was found within an ordering that helped direct social, economic, and religious life so that the person was free to pursue vocations of work and the spirit. Thus democracy came only with the acceptance of hierarchy and authority, but authority oriented toward the person and transcendence. This allowed the person to search out his own freedom, which to Maurin was the finding of vocation and working toward the common good.[8]

In May 1938, the *Catholic Worker* celebrated its fifth anniversary. The month, however, was a somber one. It had been clear for some time that the world was moving toward another global conflict, and, appropriately, the lead article was not its own celebration but a plea to attend Mass for peace sponsored by a recently organized Union Prayer for Peace. If Catholics were divided on questions of collective security, of conscientious objection and boycotts, there was one thing they could agree on: the efficacy of prayer. And the most efficacious prayer was corporate prayer.

The editorial addressed the movement's past and its aspirations for the future. In five years groups had sprung up all over the country and hospices were now located in New York, Boston, Pittsburgh, Detroit, Chicago, Milwaukee, St. Louis, England, and Australia. The paper's circulation had grown to 165,000 and it was being read not only in America but in India, China, Latin America, and all across Europe. This wide distribution of the paper and the travels of Workers across the country was done solely for the institution of Maurin's program: to give immediate relief to those in need and to work for a cooperative order.[9]

The body of the anniversary issue carried letters from various communities that, while too small to open hospices, affiliated themselves with Catholic Worker philosophy. These were called Catholic Worker Cells, and Maurin often described them as cells of good living. Each letter told of an experiment with Maurin's program. An interesting letter from a Brother Matthew in Akron, Ohio, was a meditation on Maurin's "back to the land" philosophy. Though Brother Matthew felt that singular farming communes might bring a sense of isolation and diminution of Catholic thought, the combination of village with farming life would overcome this danger. Concentration in the village would give rise to a series of guilds that based their solidarity on craft and service to the community. This form of community would usher in prayer. "I seem to see too the village Church brooding mother-like over the clustered homes—her bell softly calling all to frequent prayer." The village would exemplify all phases of Catholic life and might include a Monastic Wheel: contemplative monastery at the hub, the branches of education and work as the spokes, and the village as the rim. "All would be in a constant state of rhythmic revolution sending sparks of Catholic Action into the farmlands—which in turn, send back their produce to maintain the Living Wheel."[10]

June 1938 saw the beginning of the third summer of the farm commune at Easton. Maurin had visited the farm periodically while continuing to make his home in the city hospice (recently moved to Mott Street), and the previous summer had delivered a series of lectures on the farm entitled "The Green Revolution." This summer, however, Maurin was to do more than speak to the Easton community, he was to live and work with the community as well.

The reports from the farming commune published in the *Worker* over the past years had been mixed. Recent word had been encouraging. Though frequent rains and insufficient manpower had made work difficult, it was reported that cultivation was proceeding on schedule. Eight acres of oats and alfalfa, ten acres of corn, three acres of potatoes, and a few more acres of individual and common garden plots had been planted. Long-neglected peach and apple trees had been pruned and were loaded with fruit. Berry bushes yielded an abundance. The menu on the farm was almost totally confined to foods raised on the premises and, with few exceptions, the use of canned and prepared goods had been eliminated. Future hopes included plans to build an open-air oven for making bread, to repair shoes and make clothes, and to further reduce purchases of items that the commune could not make or grow. Members were now removing a partition in the lower house to construct a chapel where daily Mass could be said.[11]

Five months earlier, in January, Dorothy Day had written a critical review of the farm's success in the *Catholic Worker*. This was written in response to a letter Maurin had received from Carl C. Taylor, head of the U.S. Division of Farm Population and Rural Life, who had met Maurin at the National Catholic Rural Life Conference in November and was fascinated with his farm commune experiment. Echoing her earlier articles on the farm, Dorothy declared that much had been accomplished with Maurin's program in the space of three years. Although only a few of the commune members could stay through the first cold winter, over fifty people were now living and working on the farm. Dorothy reflected that many had come and joined the movement, helping both in the city and on the farm:

> They have come to us without hope and have been given hope. They have had no philosophy of labor, and they have been given a philosophy of labor. They have felt that poverty was a disgrace, and they have learned that a man is not a being judged by material standards, but by what he is as a man.[12]

Beyond providing a home and dignity for a small group, the farming commune had also brought to the attention of the *Worker*'s readers and friends the idea of farming as a way of life, as opposed to farming as an industry. Moreover, it had posed the land as a solution to unemployment, still the most pressing problem of the day.

However, these triumphs and hopes for the future were clouded by the mission of the Catholic Worker movement itself. Through Maurin's teachings, the commune members had accepted voluntary poverty and works of mercy as the basis for their work. This, in turn, had created difficulties for the progress of the farm. Lack of funds and few materials hampered building and planting, precluding planning and encouraging dissatisfaction. Out of Christian charity the commune accepted all who came in need, yet many who came could do little work and knew less about the intentions of the community. Some were openly hostile. Not wishing to be exploitative or coercive, the commune tried to induce them to work through example rather than through forced participation in Maurin's program. Thus, the great difficulty was human relations. Some had come voluntarily to the communal life, while others had been forced to it through destitution. Even the farmers often thought in terms of their own comforts at the expense of the community, and difficulties between the workers and the scholars remained. Dorothy concluded accurately that there was often discouragement and dissatisfaction.[13]

Maurin's involvement with the issues of collective bargaining and the sit-down strike in 1935–1936 had not diminished his interest in the unfolding of the experiment his ideas had helped initiate. In fact, his arrival at Easton in June had been preceded by his compilation of the works of others pertaining to life on the land, and these had been published in the *Catholic Worker* from July 1937 through January 1938. The first of these arrangements was by Alfred Grosch and carried the provocative title "Why Not a Peasantry?" The essay opened by raising the question of whether farming could be lucrative. If profit was the aim of working the land, then the answer was probably no. The person who put money into the land with the idea of monetary dividends usually ended up by losing both money and land. To avoid this negative presumption, the idea of profit had to be replaced with the idea of subsistence, a term that needed to be cleansed of negative connotations. Subsistence farming was certainly common enough to the farmer who employed the resources of the land to support family life. But subsistence farming had often been denigrated as slavery. In actuality, the employed worker himself did little more than subsist, with most income from work spent on rent, food, and clothing just for survival. On the other hand, subsistence farming could be superior to subsistence wage earning if a holding was large enough, and maintenance required only the labor necessary to satisfy the needs of the farmer rather than the surplus labor necessary to produce profits.[14]

The question of communities of subsistence farmers was not a medieval imposition on the twentieth century, and to prove this, Maurin presented an arrangement of an article by Vrest Orton that outlined a movement in Vermont to reclaim village life. Just one hundred years ago, villages that combined farming, crafts, and self-sustaining industries had dotted the countryside. Most of the industries—mills, tanneries, and blacksmith shops—had been worked by people who also owned a piece of land. The demise of these villages came with the concentration of industry in the New England cities and later in the South. With little work and a population drain to the cities, these villages essentially died out.

However, the revival of the village could occur and in Vermont this was accomplished by the teamwork of diverse citizens, including a factory president, two lawyers, a state official, several carpenters, and two school teachers. The effect of cooperation was the formation of the Vermont Guild, a nonstock, nonprofit organization that guided education and instruction in crafts and the operation of crafts and industries to sell products to support their projects. The products of the guild included dishes, benches, and tables—all made from indigenous materials—iron wrought on forges, and braided rugs. Tacked on the wall of the guild office was the motto "Not a single thing will be made that is not useful." To Maurin, this confirmed hopes that village life could be reborn, and that cooperation rather than class conflict was the direction in which to move.[15]

Still, the revival of subsistence farming in a village setting, which had become the foundation of what Maurin referred to as the Green Revolution, was far away. Maurin's arrival on the farm in June confirmed the difficulties involved and began for him a time of trial. In the next few years, Maurin saw the ideals he had dreamed and worked for tested in the crucible of the Catholic Worker life. He seems to have been aware that this marked a significant time. Part of his decision to maintain a presence on the farm was to address through personal example the dissatisfaction and discouragement Dorothy Day had written of in January.[16]

Shortly after his arrival at Easton, Maurin began to write essays on cult, culture, and cultivation, which he placed on a bulletin board each morning to encourage thought and form the basis for discussion during the day. Many of these compilations have survived and are worth quoting at some length to gain a sense of Maurin's presentations. The first summer, in particular, the essays were inspired by the Dominican Sisters of Grand Rapids, who wrote on prayer; Christopher Dawson, an English historian, who wrote on culture; and Herbert Agar, American editor and author, who wrote about the land.

CULT
HOLY MASS

1. We love God best
   when we offer a gift to Him

2. And God shows His love
   by giving us a gift, too.

3. This secret giving of gifts
   takes place at Holy Mass—

4. Holy Mass
   is the greatest act of love
   between God
   and His children.

*Dominican Sisters
of Grand Rapids*

CULTURE
ROOTED IN RELIGION

1. The central conviction
   which has dominated my mind
   ever since I began to write
   and which has increased in intensity
   during the last twenty years
   is the conviction
   that society or the culture
   which has lost its spiritual roots
   is a dying culture
   however prosperous
   it may appear externally.

2. Consequently
   the problem of social survival
   is not only
   a political or economic one.

3. It is above all things religious
   since it is in religion
   that the ultimate spiritual roots
   both of society and the individual
   are to be found.

Christopher Dawson

PETER MAURIN

1. The political problem
   is not a political problem;
   it is an economic problem.

2. The economic problem
   is not an economic problem;
   it is an ethical problem.

3. The ethical problem
   is not an ethical problem;
   it is a religious problem.

Peter Maurin

CULTIVATION

1. In terms of labor
   this means
   that a workman
   had better be free
   from a home
   because if he had a home
   he would not be
   sufficiently mobile.

2. He had better be free
   from personal responsibilities.

3. Above all
   he had better be free
   from children.

4. Landless and toolless
   vagrant as the red Indian
   his successive liv[e]hoods
   at the mercy
   of one economic law
   which we have
   basely allowed

128

PERSONALIST DEMOCRACY AND THE LAND

to take the throne, from morals
—this man has of course
the vote.

Herbert Agar

1. Two rooms and kitchenette
   is not the right place
   for the home.

2. The right place for the home
   is a homestead.

Peter Maurin[17]

Maurin also formulated a daily schedule that attempted to integrate work, prayer, and study. This schedule was placed on the wall with the essays, and was to be followed by those who came to study with him. The schedule was as follows: 5:00 to 7:00 A.M., work in the fields; 7:00 to 9:00 A.M., Mass; 9:00 to 10:00 A.M., breakfast; 10:00 to 11:00 A.M., lecture or discussion; 11:00 to 2:00 P.M., rest or study; 2:00 to 3:00 P.M., lecture or discussion; 3:00 to 4:00 P.M., cold lunch; 4:00 to 5:00 P.M., lesson in handicrafts; 5:00 to 8:00 P.M., work in the fields; 8:00 to 9:00 P.M., dinner; 9:00 to 5:00 A.M., sleep. Maurin followed this schedule himself, and anyone coming outside for discussion found him breaking stones for the road with an extra hammer standing by for others to participate in the common tasks of work and thought. Other discussions would take place on the hillside and around tables. During the time set aside for lecture and discussion, Maurin would assign a book from which a person would read out loud. The reading would continue until interrupted by someone who wished to comment on the passage and the idea would then be thoroughly explored.

Many discussions took place that summer. One afternoon, the question arose as to whether the farm should raise fruit or simply continue raising cabbages, potatoes, and tomatoes. Those opposed to raising fruit thought it an unnecessary luxury that contributed to the "indolence of the rich." Another afternoon, the discussion centered on the problem of whether food grown on the farm should be sold or given away. Some protested that they would not raise food for the "idle rich" to eat, and the consensus developed that any surplus would be given to the poor. Maurin voiced objection to canning food as an unnecessary complication of life. His view that it was unjust for people to spend hours in hot kitchens canning and preserving food when it could be avoided won approval from the women. Canning was an "out-growth of civilization," and it would be easier to eat vegetables and grains stored over the winter in cellars. Maurin also advocated regional living and the diminution of world trade. The effect of this would be to "eat what you raised and raise what you eat." At the farm this would mean doing without coffee, tobacco, and oranges.

Maurin's personal example was dynamic for those who were interested in his thought, yet the reality of the farm was that many people were not interested. More and more of the people who came to the farm were refugees from the depression, not volunteers intent on building a Catholic culture on the land. Problems were multiple: stealing and waste of valuable resources, drinking, a general lack of purpose. Maurin seemed to welcome such crises if the controversy was kept on an intellectual level so as to foster clarification of ideas and principles, rather than on a personal level where factionalism could occur. His method was to listen carefully to the topic under consideration and give his opinion, an opinion that usually searched for the common ground. Maurin never forced his own thought on anyone; despite criticism, he maintained this as an integral part of his conception of freedom. Instead of coercion, more sacrifice was called for.[18]

Dorothy Day recalled an example of Maurin's willingness to sacrifice. One summer day at Easton there was a fight over an egg, a seemingly trivial matter but one that had explosive capacity in a community with little surplus. Usually, there were enough eggs for each member of the community to have one daily, to be eaten at breakfast or lunch. On this particular occasion, Louis, an ex-soldier, put his egg aside to eat later in the day, but when he came in for lunch it was gone. Louis accused the cook of stealing it. This accusation led to a fight in which blows were exchanged and the cook ended up on the floor. Maurin witnessed the fight and was so discouraged by the violence that he spoke firmly: "Since there is not enough to go around I'll do without both milk and eggs for the rest of the summer." He did just that.[19]

Maurin could also get angry at others. At one point the situation on the farm deteriorated sufficiently, with people complaining about and even refusing to work, that he wrote an angry essay and placed it on the bulletin board.

A Catholic Worker
Farming Commune
is a farm
where Catholic Workers live in community.
To work on a farming commune
is to cooperate with God
in the production of food
for the feeding of men.
Children and invalids
cannot work
but they must be fed.
Catholic Workers
must do more than their share
so as to be able
to feed the children
and invalids.
Gentlemen farmers
and lady farmettes
are not workers
they are shirkers.
Time is a gift of God
and must be used
to serve God
by serving men.
Gentlemen farmers
don't live on the sweat
of their own brow.
Gentlemen farmers

are neither gentlemen nor farmers
and lady farmettes
are not very useful
on a farming commune.[20]

As the summer ended, Maurin began to travel again, spending much of the fall and winter of 1938–1939 wandering across the United States. Typically, his travels were a mission to spread his thought and influence to others, and at least initially he was fairly faithful in writing to Dorothy to tell her of his whereabouts. In early October he was in Iowa City, Iowa, where he spoke to students and a humanist group, suggesting that they start a humanist quarterly along the lines of the *American Review*. He spent Christmas in the mining town of Butte, Montana, where he and a friend, E. J. Seaman, donned miner uniforms in an attempt to experience the working atmosphere of the mines. Though prohibited from entering the mine itself, Maurin tried to conduct discussions among the miners after their work day. This effort failed primarily because many of the miners used this time for drinking rather than discussion. Midnight Mass was spent at a local Croatian Church, and Maurin reported that the Croatian pastor read the *Catholic Worker* faithfully and supported its positions. Also in Butte, Maurin met a Catholic student from India whose father lost a million rupees because of Gandhi's campaign to boycott imported English goods. Surprisingly, the student's father was not angry with Gandhi. "On the contrary," Maurin reported, "he says what the world needs is a Catholic Gandhi."

Moving on to Seattle, Maurin met Professor Corey, a former atheist and leftist and now dean of the School of Liberal Arts of Washington State University. Corey was in the midst of formulating an intellectual synthesis that started with science and ended with liturgy. His thought had combined with personal action, for he and his Catholic wife had adopted five children. In Maurin's viewpoint, Corey was doing as much for the Church as anyone in Seattle.

Maurin next traveled to San Francisco, where he met the wife of the dean of the Law School of Santa Clara University. She was a personal friend of the governor, as well as a writer and a speaker. She was knowledgeable about the conditions of agricultural workers and became interested in Maurin's program of "producing for use." Maurin also met the archbishop of San Francisco, who gave him $200 to help the movement. Maurin enclosed it with a letter to Dorothy Day, specifying its use for a building fund on the farm commune.[21]

By March, Maurin was in San Diego with Carrie A. Cassidy, a supporter of the Worker movement. His visit occasioned three long letters to the editors from Mrs. Cassidy, providing a vivid description of Maurin's unexpected arrival:

> When I received the news Mr. Peter Maurin was coming to San Diego, I recognized my duty to go to the bus depot to meet him and bring him to my home to lunch. There were three of us to meet him. There was no time to interest the local Knights of Columbus and see if they would get their hall for him to speak, and he would not want to speak just to three of us. I wanted to hear what he had to say, so hustled round to a friend's phone and rang up all kinds of people to be at my house at six o'clock the next evening.

Twenty came and Maurin talked for two hours, "stepping on various feet" in the process. Mrs. Cassidy commented on the evening:

> Some of these pious, well-meaning people need to meet the Truth. They need to be jerked out of their ruts which all of us get into when we feel secure in our own little circles of operating methods without knowing eternal laws and the real meaning of our religion.[22]

Dorothy Day had not heard from Maurin for some time now, and wrote Mrs. Cassidy asking her to have him write to New York. Mrs. Cassidy replied:

> Do not expect Peter to write. It is not his vocation to write the ordinary correspondence which passes between ordinary people and some unusual people. Peter uses his forces intelligently and economically.... He is not young, and

time and health and energy are too short for the nonessentials.[23]

Later during Maurin's stay in San Diego, Mrs. Cassidy wrote a poem about him.

Child of simple culture
Watching human span;
Hearing Heav'n's dictation—
Nature's gentleman.

Life among the lowly
Spirit must refine;
Peace and Truth are holy—
Root and root combine.

Timely on our pathway
Pass these men of God—
Heed, then, troubled worlding
Message from the word.[24]

On his way back east in May, Maurin dropped in unexpectedly on Bill Gauchat, who headed the Martin de Porres House of Hospitality in Cleveland. This was not the first time the two had met, nor would it be the last. Gauchat and Maurin developed a friendship around shared ideals and commitments, and Gauchat became one of Maurin's closest friends and an articulate disciple.

Gauchat's diaries recorded some of Maurin's discussions. Reversing his earlier position on the relationship of the Catholic Worker movement to Catholic Action, Maurin told Gauchat that the Worker movement was not Catholic Action but Catholic activity. He explained the distinction:

If a layman works without ecclesiastical approbation, if he makes a mistake, it is his own mistake and the Church is not injured, on the other hand if he does good, he not only helps himself, and others, but it also redounds to the honor of the Church.[25]

PERSONALIST DEMOCRACY AND THE LAND

To a question about the intricacies of running a house of hospitality, Maurin responded that the idea of personalism was simple and the questioner was trying to make it complex.

When Maurin dropped in several months later to see Gauchat, the "inveterate indoctrinations," as Gauchat termed them, continued. Maurin spoke of his plans for public addresses every three months by prominent non-Catholics who agreed with Catholics "part of the way." C. G. Paulding, former editor of *Espirit* and associate editor of *Commonweal*, was to head this speaker's bureau. Members of the group were to be called Maurin's "fellow travellers." Their talks would revolve around personalism, and it was personalism that formed the bridge of various traditions to Catholicism.

One night, after a meeting ended shortly after midnight, Gauchat and Maurin talked alone for an hour more. Maurin spoke of prestige as a good thing, for once earned it could be used for good. Gauchat addressed the problems of cooperation in the house, and Maurin suggested that a kindly paternalism was necessary until the men fully understood personal responsibility. Maurin was to leave that evening and Gauchat, noting the time was late, took Maurin to the bus station where he described a scene that was familiar to Maurin in his many travels:

> The bus terminal was crowded. This is a place where one gets a good view of the true proletariat. The clothes one sees are shabby. . . . In one corner a young hard-faced sailor is talking to a sad-eyed, cosmetic masked girl: She wears an artificial corsage. There are elderly women, a few children, many men, mostly salesmen, one fancies. And here and there a real "down and outer" stealing a rest in the waiting room.[26]

Amidst this scene, Maurin recovered his bag from the locker, opened it, and began to show Gauchat the contents— all books. McNabb's *Life of Our Savior* and Mounier's *Personalist Manifesto* were there, along with many of Maurin's own notebooks, which contained his essays. He then commenced reading one of his new essays, and, fully absorbed in the reading, forgot the time. Gauchat, however, noticed and hurried him to the bus.[27]

Maurin also visited Boston, and on this trip, too, he gained disciples. Arthur Sheehan was one of these, and a very special one. Soon after their meeting, Sheehan began to accompany Maurin on his many travels, and eventually wrote the first biography of Maurin.

Like many who came into contact with Maurin, Sheehan had first been introduced to him through his essays in the *Catholic Worker*. For Sheehan, Maurin's words were exciting: a Catholic in America questioning the "divine right of capitalism to dominate the earth." Later in 1937, in the Boston house of hospitality, Sheehan met Maurin for the second time, this time in person:

> I came into the shabby meeting room where the men of the breadline sat, humble and depressing in their anonymity, on decrepit chairs. A slight odor of flophouse disinfectant from their clothes tinged the air. In a dilapidated easy chair, sole concession to comfort in a room of prim, straight-backed chairs, a little old man was curled up in a knot, running a pencil across his lips.[28]

This was Maurin, and when he introduced himself, Sheehan was shocked to discover that he was past middle age. From his writings he had thought Maurin to be a "man of thirty-five, professorish looking, with a talent for wise-cracking phraseology." As the shock wore off he adjusted his perspective. Maurin was more than a person, for Sheehan found him to be a "whole tradition of culture, peasant, practical and pious" with a deep faith. Characteristically, a few minutes after their introduction, Maurin asked Sheehan if he had come to the Worker house to get something or to give something. Sheehan replied that he had come to help for a few days before accepting a social service job in New York, and that he was curious about the Workers' program. Maurin suggested a walk, and Sheehan reflected later that Maurin's walks, like so many other of his practices, were also a mission.

As was Maurin's wont, there was no idle discussion as the two ambled through Boston's South End. Maurin quoted Lenin, saying that there could be no revolution without a theory of revolution. If that was true for a communist revolution, it was equally true for a Christian revolution. He then spoke about labor, industrialism, and strikes:

> Strikes don't strike me. Dorothy Day wanted me to write about them but I'm not interested. Industrialism doesn't interest me. I am a peasant, a medievalist. Call me anarchist or what you will but never call me a socialist. My family has had farmlands for fifteen hundred years. I come from that Catholic Mediterranean tradition.[29]

A little uneasy, Sheehan replied that you could not go back in time. Maurin responded, "People are always telling me I can't go back. It's nonsense. They can't go ahead. They are in the blind alley of industrialism and can't go anywhere."[30]

Peter's travels continued, but by May, his letters had stopped, and Dorothy Day was concerned enough to publish an open letter in the June edition of the *Catholic Worker* asking his whereabouts.

> Not knowing where you are, the only way we can reach you is through the paper. We heard you were on your way to Commonwealth College in Arkansas and sent you a night letter, but have heard nothing from them or you. Rumors reach us from Minnesota that you told someone you would be gone another six months on a trip through the South. It's a pretty hot place in the summer. Why not put it off to the Fall. Besides we need you here. Everyone is looking forward to your being on the farm at Easton this summer.[31]

This concern for Maurin was apparently justified, for Dorothy had written him some months ago to confess that the money he had sent in for the building fund on the farm commune had been used instead for the breadline in the city. This upset Maurin because he felt that, under Dorothy's direction, the house of hospitality was receiving too much attention at the expense of the farming commune. He was adamant on this point and even considered leaving the movement. Understanding the gravity of the situation Dorothy wrote humbly:

> We were terribly broke for some months. So broke when Archbishop Spellman was appointed that we did not have the three cents to get the paper telling about it. Never were we so low. We had borrowed money from our Italian neighbors and they helped out too by sending us over their leftover food.[32]

Having sent out an appeal the month before, Dorothy assured Maurin she was in a position to restore the part of the fund that had not already been spent on the farm.

Dorothy pressed the point of the Worker movement's need for Maurin. A letter had come last week from a priest in Belgium who was in the process of writing a book about the movement, and, among other things, had asked permission to reprint some of Maurin's essays. Maurin was needed in New York to help lend direction to the movement. The Boston and Philadelphia houses had requested his presence. All twenty-six members of the Easton farm sent their love. Dorothy ended the letter pleading with him to come home soon.[33]

In the June 1939 issue of the *Catholic Worker*, Stanley Vishnewski announced that the first summer school to study the theory and history of the Worker movement would open during the month of July on the farm in Easton. Maurin, who had returned and been reconciled with Dorothy, would give a series of talks on "Current Events in the Light of History," assigning a book a week to be read and discussed. Topics would include farming communes, the cooperative movement, houses of hospitality, labor and communism. The students would be expected to participate in the work of the farm, and the month on the farm would be followed by a week of field work in New York City. In the city, students would distribute literature and visit centers of Catholic Action, as well as participate in the work of the house of hospitality. Vishnewski also included two anecdotes about Maurin. One was an incident that had occurred in the past year, when, invited to a professor's home for dinner, Maurin was mistaken by the wife for a gas meter reader and ushered down into the cellar where he remained without complaint until the professor's arrival. The other occurred at a meeting where he was introduced as Dr. Maurin and asked what university he graduated from. Maurin's reply: Union Square. He would repeat the latter story with a smile, saying that they never again referred to him as Dr. Maurin.[34]

Erwin Mooney, a student from Notre Dame who attended the summer school, published his reflections on the month in the July–August issue of the *Catholic Worker*. Mooney first related the format of each school day. Discussions were held in the mornings from 9:00 to 11:00, in the afternoon from 3:00 to 5:00, and in the evening from 7:00 to 9:00. The worker side of scholarship was not neglected, for the students pitched hay, picked cherries, and performed other chores around the farm, reminding Mooney and the others of the "dignity of work." Classes were conducted in an unusual way. One person read a chapter from a book under study, and when the reader had finished, each person had an opportunity to comment on what had been read. Discussion would ensue, and often the discussion would wander from the reading itself. Because they were not bound by the formalities of the classroom, a thorough discussion of the points raised could be pursued.[35]

With the summer over, Maurin once again embarked on a lengthy trip across the country, this time with the specific purpose of attending the National Catholic Rural Life Conference in Spokane, Washington, on October 15. This conference was an annual event, and Maurin tried to attend each year, usually bringing a younger person to travel with him. For Maurin, these conferences were a place to meet others interested in the land, as well as a place to renew old acquaintances met on previous travels.

On this occasion, Maurin brought Martin Paul, a young convert from Lutheranism who was greatly influenced by Maurin and the Catholic Worker movement in general. Typically, they stayed at flophouses on their way to Spokane and at the conference itself. Paul recalled that, in the evening, Maurin would take his only shirt, wash the collar out in the washboard with hand soap, and hang it out to dry in order to have a clean shirt in the morning. During the conference, in an informal discussion with bishops and archbishops, Maurin suddenly interjected into the discussion, "We will lead and the clergy will follow." Paul took this to mean that the laity needed to pioneer a reinvigorated Catholicism. The reaction of the bishops, and indeed most of the hierarchy, was one of respect. They recognized Maurin's devotion and the soundness of his ideas, even if they felt his Catholicism to be a little romantic.[36]

Maurin spent Christmas in St. Louis, and his presence did much to lend direction to a woman involved in her own religious search. Her name was Mignon Virginia McMenamy, and a few months before Maurin's visit she had become acquainted with the Catholic Worker house in St. Louis. The philosophy of the movement stunned her, for McMenamy had believed fully in her times, in the idea that progress was making things better and better, and in the new freedom that modernity was bringing with it. In conversation, a young Catholic Worker had dispelled this vision, and McMenamy left her former life for the Worker movement. She described her new life:

> We had round table discussions. We gave clothing away, we begged day-old bread, brewed coffee a second time; we ate strange concoctions made of whatever mixtures the restaurants had left over and gave to us. There were men who came to us to be fed who had such an odor that after one whiff we became knocked out ourselves but tried to protect visitors from so sudden a shock. Above all else we prayed the liturgical prayers of the Church together and I experienced the joy of "Christians loving one another."[37]

When Maurin arrived in St. Louis for Christmas, McMenamy was excited. She had heard him quoted over and over again, and knew that he had not only founded the Catholic Worker movement but had also inspired Dorothy Day. Still, like so many others, she was not prepared for the man she met.

> He was such a strange looking little man. Easily he could have pushed a wagon of fruit down the street, and gone unnoticed. If you did not see his eyes.
> About ten of us had supper together. This was where Peter was at his best, in a small group. I was electrified by

the flash of intellect that did not seem separate at all from the man in the way it does separate in a classroom. I had so many questions to ask, and not one of them did he fail to understand. . . . I remember especially we talked on work. Let the worker be a scholar and the scholar a worker, said Peter.

We pushed the doors open between the dining room and kitchen and a lecture was announced for the evening. There were perhaps 30 people present. I wish I could remember all that was said. Outstanding in my mind are the three who "found his saying a hard saying" and walked out in the middle. Peter had just announced in his own words St. Thomas Aquinas' "All goods are necessary, useful or superfluous." What is necessary to us we must keep. What is useful we may keep or we may give it away. What is superfluous belongs to the poor. What we take with us when we die are the things we give away.

McMenamy described Maurin at Christmas Vespers:

Peter knelt, apparently unmoved, hunched up little peasant that he was. He was at home, in his Father's house. "Notice how he is integral, how his whole man prays," Don Gallagher said to me. When we came out from Chapel most of us were silent, too awed by the beauty of what we witnessed as the nuns gave virile objective expression to their love for the newborn Christ in Gregorian Chant, to say anything at all. I did remark, "Why it was like one great violin playing." And Peter responded: "The violin is an imitation of the human voice."[38]

CHAPTER SEVEN

Final Years
1940–1949

By 1940, Maurin's warnings of the decline of Western civilization and the rise of totalitarianism had come true. The world
was now engrossed in an ideological and physical struggle for
survival. Who and what would survive this struggle? Few could
answer the question, and Maurin would not attempt to. But he
was certain where the cause of the world situation could be
found. Liberals trying to escape the death of liberal economics
in the depression had looked to the authority of the political
state; the rise of fascism had more to do with the failure of economic liberalism than with a demonic Hitler. Fascism was not
an end unto itself but was the stopgap between the chaos of
capitalism and the dictatorship of state socialism.[1]

To look only at the problem as it manifested itself was to
deal on the superficial level. For Maurin, it was not the form
that totalitarianism took, but the roots out of which it grew.
This is what defined the essential evil of its diverse manifestations. Totalitarianism was evil in that it claimed too much, and
Maurin phrased the problem in terms of the worldly and spiritual claims of Caesar. Marxists and fascists were Caesars not
satisfied with what was rightly theirs but also wanting the
things that were God's. To claim the things that were God's
was to set themselves up as gods, and these claims had to be ex-
posed and condemned.[2]

In a world experimenting with systems of total domination and global warfare, how did one expose and condemn? For
Maurin, at least, the answer was clear: by continuing to alert

the world to the foundations of the problem through clarification of thought, and by embodying the answers to these problems through witness to God and neighbor. However deep the problem, though, the specific issues of conscription and war remained before Maurin and the Catholic Worker movement in general.[3]

Years of articles and discussions among Catholic Worker people all over the country had provided little agreement on the issues of active resistance to conscription and war, but, by 1940, these issues were becoming urgent due to the deteriorating world situation. Dorothy Day addressed the issue forthrightly. Conscription and war diverted resources from productive uses and created hostility and insecurity among nations. Democracies were transformed into totalitarian war machines, blurring personal conscience in the mobilization of the masses. Conscription and war were political games, but it was the poor and innocent who suffered. Violence was the rending of the Mystical Body of Christ; conscription was preparation for this violence and war carried it out. Both needed to be opposed.[4]

In August 1940, Dorothy sent a circular letter to members of the movement throughout the country, asking them to register their position as conscientious objectors to conscription and war. Dorothy pointed out that the differences between those who wholeheartedly supported the pacifist stand and those who did not but were silent about their opposition could be reconciled. But to those who publicly opposed the pacifist stance of the Worker movement, reconciliation was impossible. Public opposition meant fundamental disagreement with the movement. Dorothy felt such dissenters should disassociate themselves from the Worker movement and discontinue the use of its name. She explained that the New York Workers had taken a consistently pacifist stand and that there was to be no equivocation or change in the future.[5]

Maurin's stand on conscription and the war was less succinctly stated than Dorothy's, and his general view of both can only be suggested through his own essays and the arrangements of works of other authors on the subjects. However, his own choice was clear, as demonstrated in his earlier refusal to accept military duty in France and in his later emulation of the life of Francis of Assisi. Both showed a deepening fear of organization and coercion and a desire to follow the counsels of perfection, one of which was a refusal to do harm against neighbor even if endangered.

As early as May 1934, Maurin had written a short essay in response to a talk given by Carlton Hayes. In it, Maurin questioned subservience of conscience to national aspirations by playing on the theme of supporting one's country regardless of the merit of its position. To stand up for your country regardless of its correctness was wrong. Sometimes, to correct that position, one had to say no. In the December 1937 issue of the *Catholic Worker*, he expanded the theme of conscience in reference to propaganda about the barbarian quality of the adversary. Indeed, in Maurin's view, the distinction between barbarians and civilized peoples was often blurred by the actions of the "civilized." If barbarians were those living on the other side of the border, the civilized were not ashamed to arm themselves for protection. And if the barbarians invaded, there was no hesitation in killing them before trying to civilize them. With this attitude, the persistence of calling one side civilized seemed ironic to Maurin. A classic example of this barbarian-civilized dichotomy was the Italian invasion of Ethiopia, ostensibly done to "civilize" Ethiopians. The Italians still retained the notion that "invaders can civilize the invaded." In Maurin's view, if Ethiopians needed to be civilized, the best way was to prepare the young men of Ethiopia for the priesthood. This example served to reinforce Maurin's major point that civilization came not through force but through religion.[6]

By April 1938, in an essay published in the *Catholic Worker* entitled "Peace Preparedness," Maurin was not only calling for physical disarmament but for disarmament of the heart. Maurin wrote:

They are increasing armaments
in the fallacious hope that they
will preserve peace by preparing for war.
Before 1914 they prepared for war and got it.
Nations have too long prepared
for war; it is about time they prepared for peace.[7]

Maurin quoted Archbishop McNicholas to the effect that governments had no fixed standards of morality and thus could scarcely settle the question of war for Christians. That Christians affirming the supreme domain of God knew the injustice of modern wars raised a very practical question: Would such Christians form a league of conscientious objectors?[8]

Maurin identified strongly with a lecture delivered by Cardinal Innitzer in Vienna, which he arranged and published in the September 1939 edition of the *Catholic Worker*. Innitzer believed the Church did not bless arms, but peace. In the Sermon on the Mount, Christ had specifically blessed the poor and those who made peace, as he declared himself as the one who brings peace. He enjoined all to make peace with each other, to love enemies, and to be perfect in imitation of God's perfection. This call to perfection was Christ's wish to refuse every way of violence. Two passages in the New Testament were conclusive: the words of Jesus to Peter, "Put back your sword in the scabbard for he who draws the sword will perish by the sword," and "I give you peace, I leave you my peace, peace be with you." These words were sufficient to prove that the Gospel excluded all violence and nothing in it could be interpreted as authorizing war.[9]

Three months later, Maurin published an arrangement of an address delivered by Eric Gill to the Council of Christian Pacifist Groups in September 1938. This address went beyond the call of conscience and the commands of Jesus to discuss the nature of modern warfare itself. Gill began by comparing modern work and war. As in work, war was made impersonal by modern machinery and weapons, which reduced the soldier to a subhuman condition. Because of technology, war was less ennobling than it was destructive and degrading. The entire structure of warfare had changed: Instead of small professional armies manned by mercenaries fighting limited engagements, war had become mass war with entire populations mobilized. The result was that the vast majority who fought and were killed were involved in a struggle about which they knew little. If war had ever had a heroic aura about it, modern warfare had none. It was not a question of heroism, justice, or defense, but of plain and simple terrorism.[10]

Other evidence of Maurin's opposition to conscription and war is fragmentary, yet interesting. Two of Maurin's closest friends and disciples, Bill Gauchat and Arthur Sheehan, refused to cooperate with the war effort, and both saw this opposition as being in concert with Maurin's position on conscription and the war. With Maurin, they viewed their stance as the choice of the counsels of perfection as a higher calling but not an absolute duty. Sheehan, who was spending a great deal of time with Maurin, understood that Maurin's pacifism was the pacifism of the early Church. At that time, Church members refused to become judges because they might have to sentence men and women to death. Larry Heaney, a friend of Maurin's, wrote to a priest in January 1942 that in regard to war, Maurin believed that the reestablishment of a rugged peasantry, with its common culture and unifying bond, would contribute much to peace. If Maurin personally opposed the war, he was also cognizant of the war's tremendous popularity. Realizing the difficulties Dorothy Day was having in her vocal opposition, Maurin counseled her that for a time silence would be better than continuing vocal opposition to war. The world was not ready to listen.[11]

The rise of fascism in Europe brought more than the question of conscription and resistance to war, for it heralded as well a renewed persecution of the Jews. On the subject of the Jews Maurin would speak often. From the beginning of his apostolate, Maurin had affirmed the connection between Judaism and Catholicism. He constantly linked the Jewish prophets and the Fathers of the Church in their concern for the poor and in the outlawing of usury. He discussed the year of the Jewish Jubilee, the fiftieth year in which debtor obligations were lifted and injustices righted, as something positive and in need of present emulation. Finally, Maurin had included the Jewish people among the theists who were central to his campaign for personalist democracy.[12]

"Let's Keep the Jews for Christ's Sake" was Maurin's first essay specifically devoted to the Jewish people, which appeared in the July–August 1939 issue of the *Catholic Worker*. The Jews were a mystery to Maurin, as they were even to themselves. Though Zionists tried to build a state in Palestine, the Jews were not a nation. Though they often characterized themselves as a race, the Jews were not a race because they had intermarried with other races. The survival of the Jewish people was similarly a mystery. Maurin was cognizant of the unique position of the Jews in history as a chosen people. Moreover, the continuing presence of the Jewish people was a reminder to the world of the coming of Christ. Maurin ended his essay with an appeal to accept Jews from Europe in the American tradition of accepting refugees. To those who were against this immigration, accusing Jews of being middlemen of which America had no need, Maurin pointed to the example of Palestine, where Jews were building up cities and developing agricultural communities as well.[13]

In his essay "Why Pick on the Jews?" published in the January 1940 issue of the *Catholic Worker*, Maurin addressed forthrightly the current accusation against the Jews: their influence on the rise of bourgeois capitalism and its attendant ills. Maurin pointed out that the theoreticians of bourgeois capitalism, Adam Smith and Ricardo, were not Jews, and that modern capitalism in Germany was the work of Bismarck and Kaiser Wilhelm, both Christians. Suspect business dealings, a prime issue against the Jews, had to be "laid to the door of Christians as well as Jews," as should the separation of business from religion, which allowed business to function in a way that caused resentment. Maurin also addressed the racial question. Having shed Jewish orthodoxy, some Jews tried to replace it with a racial identity. But if the Jews were a chosen people, they were never a superior race. On the other hand, the Nordics were neither a chosen people nor a superior race. Maurin concluded that racially minded Jews and Nordics were both a "nuisance." Returning to the theme of tradition, the essay ended with the thought that Jews taught belief in a personal God and social ethics, both of which could be used to advantage by capitalists, socialists, and fascists.[14]

Two years later, in the July–August 1941 issue of the *Catholic Worker*, Maurin published an arranged essay of Leon Bloy's thought entitled "Salvation Is of the Jews," which had clarified many of Maurin's own thoughts on the Jews. Bloy, a French novelist and pamphleteer whose hatred of the bourgeoi-

sie was matched only by his love of the poor, began by destroying the myth of Jewish wealth, a myth whose inviolability
Maurin had witnessed firsthand with the Jews he had met on
the Lower East Side. Instead of wealth, the Jewish people had
borne great suffering, including the suffering of persecution by
Christians. Bloy thought the persecution of the Jewish people
was part of a continuing crucifixion of Christ, himself a Jew.

> We forget
> or rather
> we do not wish to know
> that Our Lord made man
> was a Jew,
> the Jew par excellence,
> the Lion of Judah;
> that His Mother was a
>   Jewess
> the flower of the Jewish
>   race;
> that his ancestors were
>   Jews
> along with all the
>   prophets;
> finally that our whole
> sacred liturgy
> is drawn from Jewish
>   books.[15]

Bloy thought that the history of the Jews, because of their
perseverance through suffering, damned "the history of the human race as a dike dams a river—in order to raise its level."
The Jews were the people from whom came all the knowledge
recorded of God in the Hebrew and Christian scriptures. However, the Jews were not mere survivors deserving of accolades
for past chosenness. Now, in the hour when the world was in
the greatest need of the prophetic word, the Jews were to be
sought out. Bloy for one wanted to know why the prophetic
word was not sought from the people who gave the world the
prophets and the scriptures.[16]

As Maurin read and wrote about the mystery of the Jews,

arguing for the acceptance by the United States of all Jewish refugees, he also contemplated opening a center for the discussion of Catholic doctrine to expose non-Catholics, including Jews, to the teachings of the Church. Maurin had thought about such a center for several years as a place to remove the barriers between faiths erected by the vicissitudes of time, and to once again grapple with the fundamental question of existence, religious truth. Like the storefront in Harlem, this was to be a place for clarification of thought, to move beyond cliché and history to the innermost workings of the universe. To start such an endeavor Maurin was in need of funds, and his dinner with Michael Grace of the Grace Steamship Lines in December 1939 yielded more than three hundred dollars for rent and literature. The Discussion Center on Catholic Doctrine, as it was called, was located at 196 East Third Street between Avenues A and B. Father Krimm, a Redemptorist priest, promised to act as a spiritual advisor to any prospective converts. In January 1940, Maurin advertised his new project in the *Catholic Worker:*

I. TURNING TO THE CHURCH

1. When I was in Saint Louis
    I met a Maryknoll Father
    who had recently returned
    to the United States
    after 8 years in China
    as a Maryknoll Missionary.

2. He is pleased to see
    that non-Catholics
    in the United States
    are much more curious
    about the Catholic Church
    than they were
    before he left for China
    ten years ago.

3. While modern nations
    give the sad spectacle
    of going back on their word,

149

intelligent people
are turning to the Church
as the one moral security
left in the world.

II.   BEGINNING FEBRUARY FIRST

1. Fr. McSorley
      great friend of
      The Catholic Worker
      has always favored
      the opening of small offices
      where non-Catholics
      curious about the Church
      could receive information.

2. Such an office
      has just been rented
      by Fr. Krimm,
      a Redemptorist Father.

3. It is located at
      196 East 3rd Street
      near First Avenue.

4. It will be open
      from 2 to 5 p.m.
      and 7 to 10 p.m.,
      beginning February First.

5. Tell your non-Catholic friends
      curious about the Church
      that this office
      has just been opened
      for their benefit.[17]

The advertisement for the opening of the Discussion Center on Catholic Doctrine was accompanied by Maurin's essay "Judaism and Catholicism," an essay primarily about converts from Judaism. To the charge by a Spanish fascist that Jacques Maritain, an ardent opponent of General Franco, was a converted Jew, Maurin agreed that Maritain was a convert, but not from Judaism. Far from being ashamed, however, Maritain, in Maurin's view, would have been proud of "coming from a people who gave the Blessed Mother to the world." Maritain's wife, Raissa, on the other hand, was a convert from Judaism and proud of it. She thought that Catholicism was a completed form of Judaism, and Maurin agreed that in becoming Catholic, Raissa had kept her Judaism and added the belief in Christ that Judaism lacked, in effect becoming "100 percent Jewish."

Arthur Klyber was a Jewish convert. Born on the Lower East Side, Klyber joined the Navy and became a Catholic in Los Angeles through the good example of Catholics who did not, in Maurin's view, allow anti-Semitism to distort the message of the Church. As a result, Klyber, formerly a Jew, was now a Catholic priest. Klyber was not alone, for Maurin cited six other converts from Judaism who had become Catholic priests in America. The conclusion of the essay in referring to these converts was poignant:

> If they had remained Jews
>   they might have
>   become Rabbis.
>
> As Rabbis
>   they would be
>   commenting on the message
>   of the Jewish prophets.
>
> As priests
>   they announce
>   the good news
>   that the Messiah
>   announced by the Prophets
>   died on Calvary.
>
> As priests of Christ
>   they again offer
>   Christ's sacrifice
>   on the altars
>   of the Catholic Church.[18]

PETER MAURIN

Like the storefront in Harlem six years earlier, the Discussion Center on Catholic Doctrine was simple and destined for failure. There were few furnishings and little in the way of decorations. The afternoons and evenings were spent mostly in anticipation of visitors. A diary was kept by those who volunteered for the project to record happenings of the day and to provide a list of those who had stopped in for discussion. But visitors were sparse and the pages remained blank except for notes consisting of words of encouragement to each other. However, this situation did not dampen Maurin's enthusiasm for the venture. In September, a general invitation was again extended to Jews, Protestants, and Catholics to attend a series of informational discussions on Catholic doctrine at the center:

INVITATION

We invite
Jews, Protestants, Catholics
to attend our informal conversations at the

DISCUSSION CENTER ON CATHOLIC DOCTRINE

September: 10—Christ, A Historical Figure
17—Christ, The Messiah and Son of God
24—Christ and the Church
October: 1—Christ and the Catholic Church

First two lectures—Father Thomas F. Reilly
Next two lectures—Father John A. Krimm

Tuesday evenings, 8 o'clock
196 East Third St., N.Y.C.
(Near Avenue B)

Under directorship of
Rev. John Krimm, C.S.S.R.[19]

Once again attendance was small.[20]

FINAL YEARS

At Maurin's suggestion, Arthur Sheehan wrote to David Goldstein, a Jewish convert and the well-known director of the Catholic Campaigners for Christ, for advice on the continuation of the center. Goldstein replied immediately:

> The work among the Jews is difficult, as you know. They have an ingrained hostility towards any of their tribe who enters the Catholic Church. They can imagine only three reasons for such conversions: Desire to marry a Catholic girl; money, or insanity.... Yet I do not believe that work among them should be abandoned, especially in New York, which contains more of them than in any other city in the world.[21]

Goldstein followed with advice about methods of approaching Jews: It should first be done by priests or Catholic laymen who were born Catholics. Once interested, Jews desired to meet other Jews who had gone through the difficult process of conversion. Goldstein related that he had long been interested in coming to New York City but found it impossible to get permission from Church authorities to do so, in part because of Jewish opposition. There was no doubt, though, that thousands of Jews would be attracted to the Church if approached in the right way.[22]

The Discussion Center turned out to be short-lived, both for lack of visitors and because of the inability to secure permission from the chancellor's office to continue this apostolate. However, Maurin's understanding of the importance of conversions in general and Jewish conversions in particular continued. His essays on the Jews were reprinted several times in later editions of the *Catholic Worker* and his disciple, Arthur Sheehan, carried on this concern for the conversion of the Jews until his death in 1975.

It was Sheehan's view that Maurin had come to see the return of the Jewish people to Christ and the Church as a sign that the world would begin moving out of chaos and into its proper ordering. Was not the coming of Christ the fulfillment of the promise that God had given to his chosen ones? Did not Christ come as a Jew to his own to bring them into their eschatological fulfillment? Did not the rejection of Christ have more to do with historical circumstances than with recognition of truth? To be sure, Maurin had adopted the traditional view of the Church. To bring this message to a suffering people, though, Maurin used neither coercion nor propaganda but a personal presence to witness to a question of the utmost importance. As Sheehan pointed out quite correctly, there was no trace of anti-Semitism in Maurin's position.[23]

The failure of Maurin's discussion center did not deter him from other ventures, and his newest project was to start a clearinghouse for Catholic thought. In the fall of 1940, Maurin, along with Carl Bauer and Arthur Sheehan, visited the New Institute of Social Order started by the Jesuits on West Sixteenth Street in New York City across from Xavier High School. Meeting with Father John Delaney, head of the institute, Maurin and his friends listened to the aspirations of Father Delaney and found his thought to be quite similar to what they were going to propose. Both groups sought the development of a library on social and economic thought and a description of the work done at the institute to be used by study groups or parishes. The work would be based around the parishes, and included the creation of parish credit unions to provide financial help to married couples and cooperative activities. Maurin spoke to Father Delaney of the need for houses of hospitality to further this work and Delaney asked for more information on running such a house.[24]

Another venture Maurin embarked on with his friend Bill Gauchat was the development of a Folk School, an experiment that came to fruition in the summer of 1941 at Our Lady of the Wayside Farm in Avon, Ohio. The school combined scholarship with crafts and work on the land, and Maurin hoped that students would get a vision of a good rural culture and economy based on a subsistence rather than acquisition. Labeling the school a folk school was not insignificant, for he saw this institute accomplishing dual objectives: to teach students what a folk culture was like with its emphasis on cooperation and religion, and with this knowledge to begin moving toward the revival of such a culture. The school was well attended and the activities diverse. To emphasize the centrality of worship, an outdoor chapel was built with the altar made of fieldstone. Maurin taught Church history and Ade Bethune taught lettering; woodcarving and folk dancing were also taught.[25]

As the end of 1941 approached, the United States formally entered the war following the bombing of Pearl Harbor. Amid this turmoil, Maurin continued to reflect on the efficacy of the spiritual in transforming the human predicament. In one of his last original essays, "The Pope and the World," published in the December 1941 issue of the *Catholic Worker*, Maurin commented on Aldous Huxley's recent thoughts on the mission of theocentrists in a dissolving world. The business of the theocentrists and the "theocentric Pope" was not to capitulate to passions of war, but to tell the world that the poor remained God's concern. The need of the poor and the suffering to be fed and cared for was paramount. Though others would tell the pope to mind his own business, the pope would have to stand firm.[26]

But it was not just the pope who had to speak; the laity had to act. And for Maurin the activity of the laity was more and more bound up in the practice of poverty. Maurin's arrangement of Eric Gill's essay "On Poverty" in the December 1941 issue of the *Worker* spoke of the Christian call even during world conflict. For Gill, as for Maurin, Christianity not only was a religion of poverty; it asked believers to embrace poverty. This recommendation pervaded the life and teachings of Jesus as the son of a village carpenter, poor himself, followed by poor men and women. Adoption of poverty was not only rewarded in the future life but was the reasonable way of experiencing the material world. The way of poverty was the holy path, and the poor man was not deprived, but in the paradox of poverty thrived. The poor man did not rob others but loved others more than himself. Gill continued, "And whatever may be said about Christianity in other respects this at least is clear, crystal clear, clear as the stars: Christianity is the religion which blesses the poor." Maurin could only agree.[27]

August 1943 found Maurin and two Catholic Workers, David Mason and Janet Masu, traveling to the Alcuin farming community located in northern Pennsylvania. The journey to Alcuin was an interesting one. Here amid the mountains, Ray

Scott, a friend of Maurin's, had started a 325-acre community farm. The farming community had adopted many of Maurin's ideas, including subsistence farming and crafts, and the practice of voluntary poverty. Following Maurin, the Alcuin community saw themselves as a school of social reconstruction, and adopted much of Maurin's terminology. The revolution they proposed would be radical, personal and communitarian.

Though the community was still in the developmental stage, cooperation in the labor of the farm and participation in liturgical prayer and discussion had been achieved. There were no complete family units as yet and thus living arrangements remained communal. Houses were being built, however, and the farmwork was being accomplished. Yet the community was far from ideal, for problems of leadership and personal responsibility were also present at Alcuin. Maurin engaged Scott in many discussions, insisting, as he had ten years earlier, that they were called to be Catholic Radicals rather than Catholic Workers, and that hospices remained the interim goal to the final destination, farm communities.[28]

From Alcuin, Maurin and his friends went to Oakmont, Pennsylvania, for a retreat. In the past three years, retreats had become important in the life of the Catholic Worker movement due to the influence of Dorothy Day, who justified them by citing Maurin's emphasis on the spiritual. The retreat lasted a week and took place at Saint Anthony's Village, located on a plateau high above the Allegheny River. The "village" was an orphanage with six buildings dominated by a large school. A bronze statue of Saint Anthony greeted the retreatants in the front of the school and the area was dotted with willow trees. Seventy people attended, including fifteen women and four blacks. The retreat schedule was less than leisurely. Five hours of conferences were held daily, with each conference followed by fifteen minutes of meditation. With the exception of vocal prayers and singing, the retreat was conducted in silence.

David Mason, who reported on the retreat, was impressed with the quiet, finding that many began to realize for "the first time the great value of silence." It made possible concentration on the material presented by the retreat master and ended idle discussion. Mason was particularly interested in seeing how

Maurin adhered to the rule of silence, and reported that he was a "perfect calm all week, and those who know how much of a talker Peter is will understand how great was the abnegation involved." Remaining after dinner of the final day, Mason reported that Maurin made up for his week of silence, talking to everyone who would listen, and "that means just everyone."[29]

The retreat had clarified Dorothy Day's decision to take a year of absence from the Worker to enter into a time of solitude and reflection. For years now the movement had thrust new responsibilities on her until the burden had become so great that renewal was essential. Part of the blame for this could be laid on Dorothy herself, for her personality and strong will made her a natural leader. Her stand on issues, particularly conscription and war, made her more than ever the center of the movement. Maurin was also to blame for shifting responsibility onto Dorothy, because from the beginning Maurin had "proposed" and Dorothy "disposed." Translating Maurin's own phrasing was not difficult. While he was conducting discussions all over the country, Dorothy had the terrible task of holding the movement and the paper together, indeed even of charting their course.[30]

In the October issue of the *Catholic Worker* an editorial appeared entitled "We Carry On," signed by Maurin and by Arthur Sheehan, who, in Dorothy's absence, had become editor of the paper. They intended to carry on the work to the best of their ability: "We shall continue to work for a Christian synthesis of *cult, culture,* and *cultivation,*" the editorial stated.

> We believe that true culture must have its roots in religion. It will flourish only in an industrially decentralized society which gives to the cultivation of the land its proper place in the scheme of things and recognizes the personal right of each man to choose his own vocation and exercise it in consonance with the common good.

The aim would remain what it had been all along.

> To labor for the attainment of a society founded on Christian principles, through the program of indoctrination,

houses of hospitality, and the agricultural and industrial co-operatives which will enable men and women freely to achieve the destiny for which God created them.[31]

Though still on leave from the movement, Dorothy Day wrote an article in February 1944 for the *Catholic Worker* reflecting on what was apparent to those involved: the failure of the farming commune at Easton. Why had an experiment, begun with such hope and fervor, failed? To begin with, there had not been enough voluntary poverty. Yes, the workers had gone without salary, worn cast-off clothes, and slept in cold houses, but the tastes and desires created by advertisers remained in comforts of familiar foods, cigarettes, and movies. The adjustment from cities and urban employment to the countryside and working the land had not been easy, especially the long hours required in the planting and harvesting seasons. Poverty was also working against the community in terms of food supply, for the farming had been difficult. Dorothy pointed out that you could not eat the pig you were fattening for slaughter later, nor could you eat the chicks, hoping to use their eggs for food. Without any subsidies, voluntary poverty and asceticism were necessary, yet both were lacking in many. Those who came were neither hermits nor ascetics but refugees, the poor, the unemployed, and the bourgeois of an affluent country.

Dorothy also blamed Maurin. He was always willing to sacrifice order and success for the sake of making his point. His sayings were repeated over and over again:

> "Be what you want the other fellow to be," he kept saying. "Don't criticize what is not being done. See what there is to do, fit yourself to do it, then do it. . . . Everyone taking less, so that others can have more. The Worker a scholar, and the scholar a worker. Each being a servant of all, each taking the least place. A leader leading by example as well as by word."[32]

Leadership was also a problem. On the question of majority rule Maurin was clear: "I do not believe in majority rule. I

158

do not believe in having meetings and elections. Then there would be confusion worse confounded, with lobbying, electioneering and people divided into factions." For Maurin, the ideal rule was the rule of the monasteries with an abbot who was accepted and obeyed by his subjects and whose decisions came after consultation with them. The problem with this concept of authority was that, while it fit the monastery in demanding the responsible independence of each monk, it did not fit the farming commune where many of the people had trouble just governing themselves. When Dorothy asked Maurin if he ever became discouraged over the failures he replied, "No, because I know how deep-rooted the evil is. I am a radical and know that we must get down to the roots of the evil." In October 1944, under Dorothy's direction, the *Catholic Worker* announced the demise of the Easton farm commune and its replacement with a center for retreats.[33]

Before the year was out it was clear that Maurin's health was failing. In the summer and fall of 1944 he had been inundated with visitors, some of them mentally deranged. They would not leave him alone, and he would not excuse himself. When Dorothy Day returned to the movement in the fall, she found Maurin exhausted, his face drawn and grey. His voice was slow and he had difficulty remembering names. Dorothy took him to a doctor and pleaded with him to keep more regular hours and to turn his visitors out. Maurin replied: "But they are driven from pillar to post. None will listen to them. I was trying to find out what they were trying to say." It was Dorothy's view that Maurin had suffered a stroke. Though he would have good days and bad, Maurin never quite recovered his full health after that spring.[34]

Retired from his street apostolate, Maurin's life was hardly less arduous than before. The winters were bitter in the city and on the farm, and the unpopular stand the Catholic Worker had taken on the war made it even more difficult to raise funds for food and rent. Staying at the farm in the winter of 1945 was particularly difficult; overcoats were needed at the evening meal, served in the basement. It was during this winter of 1945 that Maurin, when being coaxed to recite one of his essays, shook his head and said that he could no longer remember them. At the same time he handed eight looseleaf volumes of arrangements of Eric Gill's works to Arthur Sheehan, saying that he had written enough. It was up to the young people now, Maurin said. When asked a question he would reply that he could no longer think.[35]

There are only scattered references to the years that followed. In the summer of 1946, Maurin's baptismal day was celebrated at Easton. A play was held in the evening and Dorothy reported that the celebration was joyous. Several of the Workers acted out three of Maurin's essays, and afterward others were read aloud. Also in June, a series of summer retreats began at Easton, most of which Maurin attended. Though his condition had not noticeably worsened, Maurin was anointed in late July as a precautionary measure, on the advice of the doctor.[36]

In March 1947 Dorothy Day went up to Rochester, New York, where Maurin had been staying for the winter with a family affiliated with the Rochester Catholic Worker, to bring him down to New York City for a visit. He withstood the journey well, but after a day in the city disappeared from the house of hospitality. The Workers were alarmed and everyone scattered in different directions looking for him. The police were called; some Workers searched the Bowery and others sat up the night worrying. Finally, everything possible having been done, the cloistered Maryknoll Sisters, the Carmelites of Newport, and Abbot Dunn of the Trappist monastery in Gethsemene were notified and asked to offer prayers for his safe return. Dorothy speculated that perhaps Maurin had become tired of being waited on, of being surrounded by love and care, and decided to go back to the Bowery to "end his days in solitude and poverty." Four days later at noon he returned. He had spent the last days riding buses, stopping in coffeehouses for soup and sleep, and being accused of a half-dozen crimes by the police. All the while he was uncertain of where he was. To make sure the episode was not repeated, it was resolved that notes containing his name and address would be put in his pockets.[37]

During the spring, the Worker movement acquired another farm, five miles west of Newburgh, New York, which Dorothy envisioned as a center for retreats and conferences. Maurin now divided his time between the new farm and the house of hospitality in New York. The main house on the Newburgh farm was too cold for him in winter, as only wood was burned in the furnace. For more warmth he moved to a rear house, a structure of poured cement built originally as a chicken coop. When Dorothy went in to see if Maurin was warm enough, she found him lying in bed with his pants folded neatly under his head and his coat wrapped around his feet. This was a habit he had acquired from living in flophouses, where clothes were often stolen. Once she found him sleeping in the dead of winter in a cold room with only a spread over him. Someone had taken his blankets.[38]

The winters continued to be difficult for Maurin and in December 1948 Dorothy again brought him down to New York City from Newburgh. There the doctor had to be called in because of Maurin's bad cough, which was diagnosed as cardiac asthma. In February, the doctor had him spend ten days in Saint Vincent's Hospital for a general checkup. He received many visitors and was reported to be "quite animated." Told about a group of worker priests in France, Maurin "glowed" and expressed the hope that factory workers would study theology in order to spread their knowledge to their fellow workers. Instead of general strikes or class war as means of reconstructing the social order, he once again affirmed the necessity of educating the workers and of keeping the long-range view of the land in mind.[39]

In May, Dorothy again reflected on Maurin's life and his poverty, which, in her view, had now become absolute.

It is hard to make our readers understand it. They read, or half read the articles that we run month after month and no matter how many times we explain that they are reprinted from much earlier issues, and that Peter has not written for four years, they write enthusiastically and tell us how they profited by his last thoughts. "His mind is as keen as ever," they say enthusiastically.[40]

But Maurin's mind was no longer keen and Dorothy thought the decline significant. After all, the only thing he had retained in his poverty had been his mind. But the last years had seen the deterioration of the interior senses, the memory and the will. When friends woke him in the morning for Mass, he struggled to get out of bed. At night for rosary and compline it was the same. His physical appearance was no better:

> He sits on the porch a huge old hulk. . . . He looks gnome-like, as though he came from under the earth. He shambles about, one-sidedly as though he had a stroke. His head hangs wearily as though he could not hold it up. His mouth, often twisted as though with pain, hangs open in an effort to understand what is going on around him. Most of the time he is in a lethargy, he does not try to listen or to understand.[41]

To Dorothy, Maurin was a victim. The things he loved most, his spiritual work, his active work to build houses, make things for the chapel, and travel about to talk of the things of God, were now gone. Incontinent and bedridden, he began his last days separated from the work and the people he loved.

On Sunday, May 15, 1949, Maurin died at the Newburgh farm in his room in the rear house. The day before there had been visitors from Canada and Europe who told Maurin all he had meant to the lay apostolate throughout the world. To Dorothy, their visit was like a "benediction from Europe." On Sunday, Maurin had been dressed and brought to Mass. After Mass he rested and Sunday night he slept restlessly. About eleven he began coughing and after several minutes he tried to rise, but fell over on his pillow, breathing heavily. Father John Faley, the chaplain at Newburgh, was called in, and prayers for the dying were said. Maurin died immediately with little struggle or pain.

On Monday he was laid out at Newburgh in the conference room where discussions and lectures had been held. Flowers were in abundance. As was his clothing during his life, his burial suit was one donated for the poor. There was no rouge on his cheeks nor any other burial amenities. A simple requiem Mass was sung in the chapel.

The next morning Maurin's body was brought to the New York City house of hospitality and laid out in the office. The room had been cleaned and painted several months earlier and so seemed fresh. People from all over the city and the country came to view the coffin. "Whenever we were sitting in the room," Dorothy Day wrote, "we saw them quietly, almost secretly pressing their rosary beads to Peter's hands. Some bent down and kissed him." Floral pieces donated by the neighbors and branches of flowering shrubs sent from the farm surrounded the coffin. Several priests came and led mourners in the rosary.

Funeral services were held at Transfiguration Church on Mott Street. Among the pallbearers were David Mason, who had traveled with Maurin, and Arthur Sheehan. The Mass was beautiful, the singing "loud and triumphant," and a sense of joy was present, "because we were sure that angels and saints joined in."

Maurin was buried in St. John's Cemetery, Queens, in a grave donated by Dominican Father Pierre Conway. The undertaker tried to sell artificial grass to cover up what he had called "the unsightly grave," but Dorothy Day refused, reflecting that she loved the sight of the earth that was to cover Maurin. "He had come from earth as we all had, and to the earth he was returning."[42]

CHAPTER EIGHT

Maurin's Legacy

The response to Maurin's death was immediate and widespread. The official Vatican paper, *L'Osservatore Romano*, commented that through "simple and expressive prose" Maurin had helped develop an important apostolate among the less fortunate. The *New York Times* printed an obituary that was simple, stating merely that from Maurin's own poverty he had come to understand the needs of the poor. *Time* magazine carried an obituary that reiterated Maurin's philosophy:

> His aim was to change modern society into one in which "it would be easier for people to be good." His message was simple and uncompromising: capitalism, with its foundations in usury and its dehumanizing of man by machine, is just as bad for mankind as socialism with its depersonalizing state. Workers, he thought, should leave the factories and work the land in agrarian communities retaining the barest minimum of private property.

Time also reported Maurin's death in a peculiarly perceptive and beautiful manner:

> Dressed in a castoff suit and consigned to a donated grave, the mortal remains of a poor man were buried last week. These arrangements were appropriate; during most of his life Peter Maurin had slept in no bed of his own and worn no suit that someone had not given away. But to his funeral among the teeming, pushcart-crowded slums of lower Manhattan, Cardinal Spellman himself sent his representative. There were priests representing many Catholic orders, and

there were laymen, rich and poor, from places as far away
as Chicago. All night long before the funeral they had come
to the rickety storefront where the body lay, to say a prayer
or touch their rosaries to the folded hands, for many of
them were sure that Peter Maurin was a saint.[1]

The themes of poverty and sainthood ran through the hundreds of letters and telegrams received by the Worker concerning Maurin's death. Jim Richter, a student at the Seminary of
the Immaculate Conception in Huntington, New York, wrote
that a Mass had been offered in remembrance of the man "who
taught us the greatness of poverty." Though Richter had never
met Maurin personally, he felt a great debt "because by his
apostolate and mission we have seen and heard his message,
and his example thunders forth over our land." John Moody, a
Wall Street financier and acquaintance of Maurin's, wrote that
Maurin was always an inspiration: "Here, indeed, I often told
myself, is one who is truly living the Christ-like life, and not
only understands what Christ meant when he said, 'Come, follow me!' but is responding to that call in his daily life and
work. Peter was a saint." Michael Gunn, who had known and
argued with Maurin over the years, used Maurin's own understanding of poverty and death to eulogize him: "When a man
dies he carries in his hands only what he has given away. Peter
gave away everything. He lived in poverty, voluntary poverty.
He died possessing nothing."[2]

In the June 1949 issue of the *Catholic Worker*, an article appeared entitled "Poverty's Progress: Lament for a Chief,"
which spoke of Maurin's life and death. John McKeon, the
writer, had known Maurin only in those last few months of his
life at Newburgh when his mind and body had already deteriorated. But even in his old age, Maurin had the power to attract
and inspire. At Mass in the chapel at Newburgh he would sit
quietly in his seat, oblivious to what was going on around him,
yet at the Sanctus he would force himself to his knees. It was a
difficult scene to watch but it provided a lesson in spiritual discipline: an old man in great pain rendering homage to his God.
McKeon found it significant that Maurin had come to the least
and to the broken, to flophouses and gatherings of the unem-

ployed, to the failures and the fanatics, those "broken on the iron wheel of our time." He had preached a mission in simple language, sometimes deceptively simple, so that it could appear foolish and childlike. However, Maurin was in a broader sense speaking to fools, "to minds weighted down by the dross of our time, the big ideas shouted from radio and forum; from newspaper and magazine, book and newsreel."

What type of man was Maurin? To McKeon, it seemed that Maurin was not an innovator. His ideas and ideals were those never realized, those of the Christian revolution that got lost in the parade of centuries past. Instead, Maurin was an agitator, and a fortunate one at that because his mission never failed him. He had never lost faith. "Count on the fingers of one hand if you can those agitators of our time who followed into their old age the ideals of their youth without taint of either cynicism or opportunism." Maurin had done more than keep his own vision, for he had also influenced others to follow him through example.[3]

Indeed, there were many who were influenced by Maurin in his lifetime, as there were to be many after his death. Foremost among these was Dorothy Day, who became acquainted with the social teachings of the Church and gained her vocation through Maurin's example and teaching. She consistently affirmed her indebtedness to him over the years, even as she herself became a central figure in the history of the twentieth-century Church. The Catholic Worker movement survived the difficulty of the war years and continues stronger and more influential than ever. The list of those affected by the movement is long and contains such notable figures as John Cogley, Thomas Merton, and Daniel Berrigan. Even those who have rejected the main tenets of Maurin's positions have been influenced by the presence of the Worker movement. Most important in this category is Michael Harrington, who became acquainted with the poor of this country in the New York house of hospitality shortly after Maurin's death. From this experience, Harrington wrote *The Other America: Poverty in the United States,* a book that awakened the social conscience of the American people and influenced Presidents Kennedy and

Johnson to pursue programs to eliminate poverty in the United States.[4]

The themes that Maurin preached and lived—the emphasis on a dynamic Catholicism, the social apostolate, and the role of the laity in social critique and reconstruction—came to fruition in the Second Vatican Council. He was one of the first Catholics to seriously entertain dialogue with Marxists, a dialogue that is being pursued with new vigor today. His understanding of hospitality as a Christian obligation flourishes today, especially in the works of the contemporary theologian Henry Nouwen. Maurin's belief that decentralized political authority and simplicity of life provide not only the necessities for living but the context for search and freedom have similarly experienced a resurgence in recent years. These beliefs are exemplified in E. F. Schumacher's popular book *Small Is Beautiful: Economics As If People Mattered.* So, too, Maurin's understanding of the Christian mission as a witness to faith and justice in a secular world has become for many the center of their faith. Involved here is Maurin's insistence on the role of faith and tradition in providing the context for the nurturing of the person and the social order, and the way of poverty and simplicity as a sign of judgment on a world in pursuit of affluence. Even Maurin's dreams of the movement back to the land has continued in small experimental communities in New York, West Virginia, and dozens of other places around the country.[5]

But if Maurin's program has gained adherents, in the larger world his thought and program have been controversial and more often dismissed. To many, the plan Maurin wanted to move toward and felt that as a society we *had* to move toward to recover spirit and community, the return to the land, seemed then and seems today unrealistic. The question that Paul Hanly Furfey posed in 1939 in a series of articles in the *Catholic Worker* remains: Is agrarianism, and those who espouse it, romantic both in content and possibility? Does it not reflect a bias against city life and a diversion from the necessary reforms of a permanently urban civilization where most people will make their lives? Maurin's critique of industrialism, with its alienation of labor and the loss of personality in organized and bureaucratic processes, has similarly come under attack. The question that John Cort posed in 1948 in a series of articles in *Commonweal* is relevant: Is it not true that urban-industrial life, with all its faults, can be humanized, even Christianized, through organization that has as its ends the person and justice? The problem of population growth is important here as well: Can a worldwide village economy with subsistence agriculture and crafts support a population curve that grows exponentially and has already surpassed the four billion mark? Just as difficult is the predicament of religious traditions: Is the form of religiosity that nurtured Maurin and others of his persuasion available to those who must struggle in the present?[6]

There is no denying the perhaps insurmountable difficulties involved in moving from a secular, urban-industrial society to a rural-village culture rooted in faith, even if that were desired by a majority of people. Maurin, in thought and experience, could hardly deny these difficulties. However, the criticism that Maurin's vision represented little more than a romanticized version of the Middle Ages is equally difficult to sustain. To be sure, Maurin's recitation of secular and Church history suffers when compared with the complexities of post–World War II historical investigation. An example of this is his understanding of the development of cities, which he thought had much to do with the Enlightenment but probably had more to do with the development of agricultural technology that created a surplus of laborers in the countryside. Another example was his understanding that the Church had functioned as a protector of the Jews through the ages. On the other hand, his vision of reality was hardly romantic. If Maurin's hope that personal and community witness could redirect, even dismantle the power of modernity seems naive, his vision of the new social order was not superficial. If anything, Maurin was willing to confront what contemporary society labors so hard to forget and does so at its own peril: the need for meaningful work; the development of the interior life; the connection between purpose and the mysteries of life found on the land and in worship; the necessity of community; the reality of death.

In the final analysis, Maurin was in the unenviable position that all those who oppose the present find themselves in: To oppose the present is to propose a reality that by definition does not as yet exist. However, Maurin compounded the problem by proposing as a future a society that had imperfectly existed in the past. This rendered his vision less accessible to the modern imagination, used to seeing the future, progressive or not, as an extension of the present. The passivity of the modern imagination made it easier to contemplate as a future the horrific anti-utopian writings of Aldous Huxley in *Brave New World* and George Orwell in *Animal Farm* and *1984* than to imagine what was by contrast a radically human vision of the future proposed by Maurin.[7]

For that was what Maurin was addressing: not how the present was to be reformed or how the future was to be an extension of the present, but the need for a radical departure in order to ensure a future that could honestly be called human. To the complex questions of agrarianism and industrialism, Maurin replied with his own questions. Were material affluence and sense desire the ends of life or was involvement in the spirit and renunciation in serving the goal? Did the pursuit of affluence lead to the inevitable spread of affluence to others or to more and more destitution? Were the foundations of freedom and community found in individual rights to pursue career and self-fulfillment or were freedom and community found in the obligations of faith and service to neighbor? Did the pursuit of individual rights lead to granting these same rights to others or to the hoarding of rights vis-à-vis others? Did not the increasing organization of personal and institutional life to pursue affluence lead in its final form to totalitarianism on the left and the right? Was the function of the social order to ease the pursuit of materiality or to nurture souls bound for eternity? Maurin's most radical reversal of all was his understanding of poverty: to the world a sign of shame; to Maurin a sign of fidelity and salvation.

In a perceptive and dialectical manner, Maurin evolved a program that continually raised the most radical questions of personal and corporate life. By binding the fortunate to the poor and the poor to the fortunate in hospitality (remembering that his plan was that every home would have a room for the wanderer and afflicted and every parish a hospice), Maurin profoundly challenged personal *and* social conscience as if they were one. By deeming it worthwhile, even salvific, to care personally for those whom society had abandoned, Maurin challenged *every* abstract and institutional way of dealing with the afflicted. However, to care for others at a personal sacrifice was not only to challenge social and economic systems. It was to challenge the person's and the culture's perception of time and progress, the very meaning of personal and corporate existence.

Provided with this context of suffering and service, discussions for the clarification of thought could be neither cynical nor naively hopeful. And because the hospices served to catalyze personal and social conscience, the powers of the day, which in other contexts seemed so overwhelming, were demystified and fell to insignificance. It would be confirmed over and over again: After involvement in Maurin's hospices one could neither feign ignorance nor remain indifferent. If the poor were no longer abstractions in the social sense, the self was no longer immune to suffering, either its own suffering or to the suffering of others. It was this suffering that brought the person and the society closer to the source of their origins, toward the mystery of a God made man who suffered to redeem.

Perhaps this was Maurin's most prophetic and disarming (if you like, simplistic) quality. He took so seriously the question of salvation that he thought personal and social life had to be oriented around it. To give up what was superfluous, to honor the least by becoming the servant of all, to live personal and community life centered on the spiritual, was to enter into the message of salvation as preached by Christ. The terms "romanticism" of the land and "evil" of urban life were peripheral to this salvific message. The question was what form of life nurtured this message and what diverted attention from it. Clearly, for Maurin, contemporary life, with its urban-industrial base, organizational propensities, and search after affluence, hindered rather than nurtured humankind's quest for salvation. It was Maurin's great belief in human freedom to respond to the message of salvation that allowed him to think that once the message was posed, personal and community life could *and* would be shared around this message.

If many disagreed with Maurin's answers, his perception that at the heart of personal and community life was the quest for meaning and certainty could hardly be denied. The capitalist and state socialist systems that Maurin so often criticized did not claim less than the fulfillment of this human longing, albeit in secular forms. That in the coming of modernity, eschatology had shifted from the eternal to the temporal was something Maurin, in his life of wandering and reflection, could understand but not accept. His final conclusion was that the Church, in concert with others of differing faiths, had the resources past and present to carry on the struggle for eternity against the forces of modernity. Maurin knew that the struggle would not be easy and that his program of round-table discussions, houses of hospitality, and farming communes was a beginning that would often meet with failure. The move toward the world of spirit lived out in daily life would require an immense clarification and a *metanoia* of unparalleled dimensions. Maurin would call it an age of order.

> If we make
> the right decisions
> in the age of chaos
> the effect of those decisions
> will be a better order.
> The new order brought about
> by right decisions
> will be functional
> not acquisitive;
> personalist,
> not socialist;
> communitarian,
> not collectivist;
> organismic,
> not mechanistic.
> The thing to do right now
> is to create a new society
> within the shell of the old

171

with the philosophy of the new,
which is not a new philosophy
but a very old philosophy
a philosophy so old
that it looks like new.[8]

NOTES

INTRODUCTION

1. Gil Elliot, *Twentieth Century Book of the Dead* (New York: Scribners, 1972), pp. 1–15, 83.

2. Ibid., pp. 189, 190.

3. Albert Camus, *The Rebel: An Essay on Man in Revolt*, trans. Anthony Bouwer (New York: Knopf, 1956), p. 4.

4. Ibid.

5. Richard L. Rubenstein, *The Cunning of History: Mass Death and the American Future* (New York: Harper and Row, 1975), pp. 2, 4, 96. Rubenstein comments: "The destruction process required the cooperation of every sector of German society. The bureaucrats drew up the definitions and decrees; the churches gave evidence of Aryan descent; the postal authorities carried the messages of definition, expropriation, denaturalization, and deportation . . ." (4). On this movement toward mass death, see also Lewis Mumford, *The Transformations of Man* (London: George Allen and Unwin, 1957), p. 124.

6. John Murray Cuddihy, *The Ordeal of Civility: Freud, Marx, Lévi-Strauss, and the Jewish Struggle with Modernity* (New York: Dell, 1974), pp. 3–14. For the major theorist of modernization as a process of differentiation, see Talcott Parsons, *Sociological Theory and Modern Society* (New York: Free Press, 1967), pp. 192–220; 385–422; 466–520.

7. A recent example of this literature of crisis is Christopher Lasch's *The Culture of Narcissism: American Life in an Age of Diminishing Expectations* (New York: Norton, 1978), which is essentially a critique of popular culture but provides few answers to the problems it raises. A more profound discussion of the "progress and tragedy" dilemma is Rubenstein's *Cunning of History*, which ends on the somber note of attempting to keep the metropolis from becoming necropolis again. The question being raised is the transformation that is inevitable and a necessity; the movement from a literature of crisis to a literature of affirmation.

8. Johannes B. Metz, "The Future in the Memory of Suffering," *Consilium* 36 (1971): 15.

9. Abraham Heschel, *The Prophets* (New York: Harper and Row, 1962), pp. 1–26. See also Gerhard Von Rad, *The Message of the Prophets* (London: SCM Press, 1968), and Martin Buber, *The Prophetic Faith*, trans. Carlyle Witton-Davies (New York: Macmillan, 1949).

10. Simone Weil, *Waiting for God*, trans. Emma Craufurd with an introduction by Leslie A. Fiedler (New York: G. P. Putnam's Sons, 1951), pp. 98–99.

11. The idea of exile here is also undergoing a transformation, one similar to the transformation of prophet-saint. The people who comprise this exilic community are participating in one of the oldest traditions in the West: to be with the least, to suffer as a witness to injustice, and to build among the refugees and outcasts a new community. This new community, which attests to spirit and the human prospect, is breaking down the barriers that language and history have erected.

12. Edward S. Shapiro, "Decentralist Intellectuals and the New Deal," *Journal of American History* 58 (March 1972): 138–157; Cuddihy, *Ordeal of Civility*, p. 9.

13. See Martin Buber, *Paths in Utopia*, trans. R. F. C. Hull with an introduction by Ephraim Fischoff (Boston: Beacon Hill, 1949), and Mahatma Gandhi, *All Men Are Brothers* (New York: Columbia University Press, 1958).

CHAPTER ONE
1. Maurin spoke and wrote little of his life in France. What we do know comes from the following sources: from Maurin's own brief description of his early years in France quoted in Dorothy Day's *The Long Loneliness: The Autobiography of Dorothy Day* (New York: Harper and Brothers, 1952), pp. 175–177; through correspondence with Maurin's brother, Rev. Norberto Bautista, sister, Marguerite Maurin, and Father Agnel Isidore, Christian Brother Archivist in Rome, Italy, by Brendan Anthony O'Grady, found in the appendices of his study "Peter Maurin, Propagandist," (Ph.D. diss., University of Ottawa, 1954), and correspondence with Rev. Norberto Bautista and Marguerite Maurin by Arthur Sheehan, found in the Dorothy Day–Catholic Worker Collection (DD-CW), Series W-15, Box 3, Arthur T. and Elizabeth O. Sheehan Papers (Sheehan Papers), Marquette University Archives, Milwaukee.

2. Rev. Brother Norberto Bautista, F.S.C., to Brendan Anthony O'Grady, October 6, 1952, in O'Grady, "Peter Maurin, Propagandist," app. 2, p. 295; Bautista to Arthur Sheehan, January 12, 1956, Sheehan Papers, Series W-15, Box 3. Maurin described the family diet, "We did not eat calves, we sold them. We ate salt pork every day. We raised no hops, and there was no beer. We raised no grapes, so no wine. We had very little meat. We had plenty of bread—there was a communal oven. We had plenty of butter; we had eggs. We had codfish from the Brittany fisherman.... We had vegetable soups, salads and cheese." Quoted in Day, *The Long Loneliness*, p. 176.

3. Ibid.; also Marguerite Maurin to Arthur Sheehan, June 5, 1958, Sheehan Papers, Series W-15, Box 3.

NOTES

4. Bautista to O'Grady, October 6, 1952. For the spiritual life found in the Christian Brothers' schools see Jean-Baptiste de La Salle, *The Conduct of the Schools of Jean-Baptiste de La Salle*, trans. F. de la Fontainerie (New York: McGraw-Hill, 1935).

5. Arthur Sheehan, *Peter Maurin: Gay Believer* (New York: Hanover House, 1959), p. 45

6. Father Agnel Isidore to O'Grady, August 23, 1952 in O'Grady, "Peter Maurin, Propagandist," app. 1, p. 295; Sheehan, *Peter Maurin*, p. 49.

7. Bautista to O'Grady, October 6, 1952; Bautista to Sheehan, January 12, 1956; Sheehan, *Peter Maurin*, pp. 49–51.

8. Isidore to O'Grady, August 23, 1952; Sheehan, *Peter Maurin*, p. 56.

9. For the clash between the Church and the government of France see Malcom O. Partin, *Waldeck-Rousseau, Combes and the Church: The Politics of Anti-Clericalism, 1899–1905* (Durham: Duke University Press, 1969), pp. 115–188. For the beginning of *Le Sillon* see Charles Breunig, "The Sillon of Marc Sangnier: Christian Democracy in France (1894–1900)" (Ph.D. diss., Harvard University, 1953) pp. 98–151.

10. Isidore to O'Grady, August 23, 1952; Bautista to O'Grady, October 6, 1952; Bautista to Sheehan, January 12, 1956. Maurin would say of *Sillon*, "It had nothing to do with the decentralist movement, no, but it was interested in ethics. It understood the chaos of the time. . . . They were looking for an ideology. They were preoccupied about the idea of an elite in democracy" (quoted in Day, *The Long Loneliness*, p. 177).

11. For the diversity of Catholic movements in France at the turn of the century see Matthew H. Elbow, *French Corporative Theory, 1789–1948: A Chapter in the History of Ideas* (New York: Columbia University Press, 1953), pp. 81–120, and John McManners, *Church and State in France, 1870–1914* (London: PSCK, 1972), pp. 64–117. The following analysis takes issue with Anthony W. Novitsky's "The Ideological Development of Peter Maurin's Green Revolution," (Ph.D. diss., University of New York at Buffalo, 1976), in his chapter "Maurin and Reactionary Social Catholicism," pp. 170–234. While reciting the history of what he describes as "reactionary" Catholic thought in France the two people whom Maurin cited as having influenced him are discussed in a cursory way. If anything, Harmel and Sangnier were "progressive" French Catholic thinkers for their time and are identified as such by the major historians of the period in question. See, for example, Adrien Dansette's chapter "Social Catholicism and Christian Democracy (1879–1901)" in his *Religious History of Modern France*, vol. 2, trans. John Dingle (New York: Herder, 1961).

12. For a detailed description of the Harmel spinning plant see Leon Harmel, *Manual d'une corporation chrétienne* (Tours: Alfred Mame et Fils, 1879). Maurin's approval of Harmel's understanding of authority and property to serve the worker and the community is found in Maurin's essay "The Sit-Down Technique," *Catholic Worker*, April 1937, p. 1. Hereafter the *Catholic Worker* newspaper may be cited as *Worker*. For Sheehan's discussion of Maurin's interest in Harmel see Sheehan, *Peter Maurin*, pp. 52–53.

13. Breunig, "Sillon," pp. 192–249. Also see Adrien Dansette, "The Rejuvenation of French Catholicism: Marc Sangnier's Sillon," trans. James A. Corbett, *The Review of Politics* 15 (January, 1953): 38–39; for Maurin's participation in the activities of *Sillon*, see Bautista to O'Grady, October 6, 1952, and Sheehan, *Peter Maurin*, pp. 59–66.

14. Breunig, "Sillon," pp. 250–353; Dansette, "Rejuvenation of French Catholicism," pp. 44–52.

15. Maurin, "Christianity and Democracy," *Worker*, January 1941, p. 7.

16. Bautista to Sheehan, January 12, 1956.

17. Dorothy Day has suggested that Maurin's attraction to the land in Canada may have been because of the urban poverty he witnessed in his years as an activist in Paris. See Day, *The Long Loneliness*, p. 178. Whatever the reason, it is clear that Maurin had been reflecting on his own life and the world around him in making the decision to emigrate, and opting for the land was not simply a return to his peasant upbringing.

CHAPTER TWO

1. As with the details of Maurin's life in France, information on his wanderings in Canada and America is similarly scarce. Only three sources for information pertaining to these years are available: the handwritten, unpaginated notes of an interview of Maurin by Thomas Barry ca. 1936 entitled "Peter Maurin," DD-CW, Peter Maurin Papers (Maurin Papers), Series W-10, Box 1; an interview with Maurin by Joseph A. Breig, "Apostle on the Bum," *Commonweal* 28 (April 29, 1938): 9–12; and letters from Julia S. Leaycraft to Brendan Anthony O'Grady found in the appendices of his study "Peter Maurin, Propagandist," (Ph.D. diss., University of Ottawa, 1954), pp. 302–303.

2. Barry, "Peter Maurin"; Breig, "Apostle on the Bum," p. 9.

3. Ibid. Barry, "Peter Maurin."

4. Ibid.; Bautista to Sheehan, January 12, 1956, Sheehan Papers, Series W-15, Box 3. One picture survives of Maurin from the years that he taught French in Chicago and his suit attire suggests a modicum of affluence. See DD-CW, Series W-8, Box 1 (Photographs). Other evidence is noted in Barry, "Peter Maurin."

5. Dorothy Day, "Peter Maurin," unpublished manuscript, p. 241, DD-CW, Series D-3, Box 2.

6. Breig, "Apostle on the Bum," p. 10; Julia S. Leaycraft to O'Grady, July 30, 1953, in O'Grady, "Peter Maurin, Propagandist," app. 3, pp. 302–303; Barry, "Peter Maurin." The influence of Francis of Assisi on Maurin's life will be discussed in detail in Chapter 3.

7. Leaycraft to O'Grady, July 30, 1953.

8. Peter Maurin, "Human Rehabilitation," *Worker*, November 1934, p. 3; Breig, "Apostle on the Bum," p. 10.

9. Scully to Day, September 29, 1933, DD-CW, Series W-10, Box 2.

10. Arthur Sheehan, *Peter Maurin: Gay Believer* (New York: Hanover House, 1959), p. 88.

NOTES

11. Maurin quoted Popes Leo XIII, Pius X, Benedict XV, and Pius XI on the need for the Third Order to act in his essay "The Case for Utopia," *Worker*, April 1934, p. 3.

12. Barry, "Peter Maurin"; Dorothy Day, *The Long Loneliness* (New York: Harper and Row, 1952), p. 179.

13. Sheehan, *Peter Maurin: Gay Believer*, p. 89; Day, *The Long Loneliness*, pp. 170–173.

14. The biographical information on Dorothy Day is taken from her autobiographical *The Long Loneliness*, pp. 149–175, and *Loaves and Fishes* (New York: Harper and Row, 1963), pp. 3–13, and from William D. Miller, *A Harsh and Dreadful Love: Dorothy Day and the Catholic Worker Movement* (New York: Liveright, 1973), pp. 33–45.

15. Day, *The Long Loneliness*, pp. 149–150.

16. Dorothy Day, *From Union Square to Rome* (New York: Sheed and Ward, 1939), p. xiii.

17. This essay appeared in the *Worker*, May 1933, p. 1.

18. Day, *Loaves and Fishes*, p. 13. For Maurin's unpublished digest of Kropotkin's *Field, Factories, and Workshops*, which was essentially a verbatim transcript of Kropotkin's original but taken from different parts of the book and put in Maurin's poetic style, see Maurin, "Fields, Factories & Workshops," Maurin Papers, Series W-10, Box 3. Maurin also read Kropotkin's *The Conquest of Bread* (London: Chapman and Hall, 1906) and *Mutual Aid: A Factor of Evolution* (New York: Knopf, 1918).

19. Maurin to Day, April 3, 1933 in O'Grady, "Peter Maurin, Propagandist," app. 4, pp. 305–306. Maurin wrote Day another letter later that month, on April 26, 1933, with more information on how to spread their message (ibid., app. 4, pp. 307–308).

CHAPTER THREE

1. "To Our Readers," *Worker*, May 1933, p. 4.

2. Dorothy Day, *Loaves and Fishes* (New York: Harper and Row, 1953), p. 24; "Maurin's Program," *Worker*, June–July 1933, p. 4.

3. Peter Maurin, "Easy Essays," *Worker*, May 1933, pp. 1, 8.

4. "Maurin's Program," *Worker*, June–July 1933, p. 4.

5. Maurin, "Easy Essays," *Worker*, June–July 1933, p. 1; 1933, p. 4; idem, "To the Bishops of the U.S.," *Worker*, October 1933, p. 1; idem, "Back to Christ!—Back to the Land!," *Worker*, November 1935, pp. 1, 8.

6. Maurin, "Maurin's Program," *Worker*, June–July 1933, p. 4; idem, "To Our Readers, Notice! Round Table Discussion," *Worker*, December 15, 1933, p. 8.

7. "Round Table Meeting Discusses Plans for New Social Order," *Worker*, July–August 1933, p. 6.

8. "Communists Oppose Round Table Sponsor," *Worker*, September 1933, p. 12.

9. Maurin, "To the Bishops of the U.S.," *Worker*, October 1933, p. 1.

10. Ibid.

11. "Co-operative Apartment for Unemployed Women Has Its Start in Parish," *Worker*, December 15, 1933, pp. 1, 5.

12. Maurin, "Hayes of Columbia Gives Opening Night Lecture of Catholic Workers' School," *Worker*, February 1, 1934, pp. 1, 6; "Catholic Workers' School Program, 436 East 15th Street, N.Y.C.," *Worker*, February 1, 1934, p. 4.

13. *Daily Catholic Worker*, no. 2, n.d.

14. Ibid., no. 5, n.d. Opposing views were frequent and vocal, and Maurin welcomed them as contributions to further clarification. Albert Bingham, editor of the political weekly *Common Sense*, spoke at the Worker School advocating the formation of a third political party, a strategy with which Maurin could not agree, preferring, as he did, social over political action. Another night, John B. Erit, of the Engineers and Contractors Commissary Service in New York, spoke on banking and disputed Maurin's understanding of usury. In a letter to Maurin after his talk, Erit concluded that, while the Church's teaching outlawed usury, it did not condemn interest itself. The Holy See had negotiated loans and bond issues in London and other financial centers on which interest was paid and collected. Banking organizations in Italy, some of which had been established by the Church, were in Erit's mind "sufficient to prove the Church is not against banking and all lawful related endeavor which compromises paying or receiving [i]nterest etc. . . ." This challenge to Maurin's understanding having been stated, Erit confirmed room for disagreement and his hope for further cooperation. The letter itself was addressed with respect "To the modern Crusader for the New Jerusalem Peter Maurin" (Erit to Maurin, February 5, 1934, Maurin Papers, Series W-10, Box 3).

15. Maurin, "Easy Essays," *Worker*, May 1933, pp. 1, 8. See also idem, "To National Recovery Act Administration Officials—Is Inflation Inevitable?," *Worker*, December 15, 1933, pp. 1, 8, and idem, "Peter Maurin Says Usurers Are Not Gentlemen!," *Worker*, October 1934, p. 3.

16. Idem, "Easy Essays," *Worker*, September 1933, pp. 1, 12; idem, "To the Bishops of the U.S.: A Plea for Houses of Hospitality," *Worker*, October 1933, p. 1. Beyond his critique of a society based on consumption and profit, Maurin also expressed other concerns regarding modern economy. At the core of contemporary economics was an industrial model based on mass production and mass distribution. Fluctuations of supply and demand endemic to an industrial economy encouraged a cycle of inflation, unemployment, and overproduction. This Maurin saw as inextricably linked with the demise of capitalism, the appeal of state socialism, and finally the rise of fascism. If mass production and its attendant ills of unemployment and inflation encouraged totalitarianism, they likewise diminished the value of the laborer. Following Marx, Maurin saw the work of modern laborers as alienated and relegated to the status of a commodity. This alienation of the worker diminished prospects for human community, which Maurin viewed as intertwined with the dignity of manual labor found in a functional economy. (Maurin, "Is Inflation Inevitable?," *Worker*, July–August 1933, p. 8).

NOTES

17. Maurin, "For Catholic Action," *Worker*, June 1, 1934, p. 5.

18. Maurin, "Institutions vs. Corporations—Catholic Tactic," *Worker*, December 1935, pp. 1–2.

19. Dorothy Day, *House of Hospitality* (New York: Sheed and Ward, 1939), pp. 71–72.

20. Maurin, "Idle Hands and Idle Lands," *Worker*, February 1936, p. 1.

21. Maurin, "A Question and an Answer on Catholic Labor Guilds," *Worker*, February 1, 1934, p. 8; idem, "Utilitarians, Futilitarians, Totalitarians," *Worker*, June 1937, p. 1. Class warfare was an example Maurin used to demonstrate that progress had not been made in the critique of capitalism by socialists. Instead of harmonizing contacts among different classes of people in order to work toward a common future, socialists believed the polarization of the classes was the road to a just society. Maurin thought that one form of violence, the exploitation of labor, was merely being replaced by another, the pursuit of enmity between classes, and that once started, the cycle of violence could not end. Another example he used in this analysis was the establishment of a strong state and the entrenchment of dictatorship in socialist countries, both of which Maurin saw as a logical extension of failed capitalism rather than a movement toward a just and personal society (see Maurin, "Against Class War," *Worker*, August 1937, p. 4).

22. Day, *House of Hospitality*, p. 72.

23. Maurin, "An Open Letter to Father Lord, M. Ag. (Master Agitator)," *Worker*, October 1933, p. 8.

24. Ibid., December 15, 1933, p. 5. Over the years Maurin wrote two more open letters to Lord. See Maurin, "A Message to the Catholic Action Summer School," *Worker*, September 1934, pp. 1, 6; and idem, "Open Letter to Father Lord, S.J.," *Worker*, October 1936, p. 8.

25. Maurin, "The Spirit for the Masses," *Worker*, October 1933, p. 2.

26. This relationship of faith and obligation was to be one of the keys of Maurin's philosophy, a philosophy that would clearly separate him from other contemporary secular social reformers. If political movements since the French Revolution had revolved around the securing of rights for the individual through government, Maurin proposed shifting the question from the temporal to the spiritual realm. The problem of relying on the temporal order was that shifting political leadership moved various groups in and out of power. The rights of individuals would thus be dependent on the constant assertion of interest and power. By admitting to the fluctuations in power and the resulting injury to individuals, this in some sense proposed the person as a being wholly in time and history. Maurin thought this mistaken. The person, while existing in time and history, also had life outside of this process: the soul of the person was linked less with the temporal than with the eternal. In effect, the person was embarked on a spiritual journey, and therefore the function of the social order was to protect and nurture the soul's journey toward the mystery of God. It was not a matter of granting rights but of recognizing the obligations of faith to pursue the spiritual and to nurture others in that pursuit as well. Maurin, "Communist Action in Schools

Challenge to Catholics, Declares Peter Maurin," *Worker*, July–August 1934, p. 3).

27. Maurin, "Christ the King Alone Can Reconstruct the World: The Practice of the Seven Corporal and Seven Spiritual Works of Mercy Is Basis of Christian Society," *Worker*, October 1934, pp. 1, 6.

28. Maurin, "A Message to the Catholic Action Summer School," *Worker*, September 1934, p. 6; idem, "A Letter to John Strachey and His Readers," *Worker*, April 1935, p. 8; idem, "Not Jewish Wealth But Irish Culture," *Worker*, December 1940, pp. 1, 4.

29. Jacques Maritain, "On the Use of 'Pure' Means," arranged by Peter Maurin, *Worker*, January 1935, p. 5; ibid., March 1935, p. 4. Maurin published one other compilation of Maritain's work; see Maritain, "The Twilight of Civilization," arranged by Peter Maurin, *Worker*, January 1940, p. 3. Maurin read many of Maritain's works, including *The Things That Are Not Caesar's*, trans. J. F. Scanlan (New York: Scribners, 1931); *Freedom in the Modern World*, trans. Richard O'Sullivan (New York: Scribners, 1936); *True Humanism*, trans. Margot Adamson (New York: Scribners, 1938); and *The Twilight of Civilization*, trans. Lionel Landry (London: Sheed and Ward, 1943).

30. Maurin, "For Catholic Action," *Worker*, June 1, 1934, p. 5. Maurin referred to this as a "sociology that had something to do with theology." Exemplars of Catholic sociology were Francis of Assisi, Thomas Aquinas, and Thomas More.

31. Maurin, "For Catholic Action," *Worker*, June 1, 1934, p. 5.

32. Henry B. Sullivan to the Editor, *Worker*, July–August 1934, p. 2; editors to Sullivan, July 9, 1934, DD-CW, Series W-2, Box 1; editors to Reverend Paul Stroh, July 30, 1934, DD-CW, Series W-2, Box 1. To a letter from a Mr. Mayer expressing a similar criticism, Dorothy Day responded apologetically: "I went over the matter with Peter at great length and he realizes the impatience of his disposition. God knows we all believe the clergy the salt of the earth and Peter gets so rabid because he always is rabid about ideas. Therein lies his strength. But after all yo[u] can criticize militarism without mentioning Father Hogan, and the N.R.A., without mentioning Father McGowan, etc. I realize that I too have often been at fault with impatience and I beg your prayers for us all to guide and guard us" (Day to Mayer, September 12, 1934, DD-CW, Series W-2, Box 1).

33. "Is Political Action an Answer?" *Worker*, June 1, 1934, p. 6.

34. "A Question and an Answer on Catholic Guilds," *Worker*, February 1, 1934, p. 8.

35. "Michael Gunn's Answer to Maurin on Catholic Labor Guilds," *Worker*, March 1, 1934, p. 8.

36. Dorothy Day, "Days with an End," *Worker*, April 1, 1934, p. 3.

37. Johannes Jorgensen, *Saint Francis of Assisi*, trans. T. O'Conor Sloane (New York: Longmans, Green, 1921); G. K. Chesterton, *St. Francis of Assisi* (New York: George H. Doran, 1924). The encyclicals concerning St. Francis that Maurin read and quoted from are as follows: Leo XIII, *Concerning St. Francis and the Third Order* (1882); Leo XIII, *Revising the Rule of the Third Order*

NOTES

Secular (1883); Pius X, *On the Corporate Activity of the Third Order* (1912); Pius XI, *On the Purpose and Mission of the Third Order* (1923); Pius XI, *On the Seventh Centenary of the Death of St. Francis* (1926). These were compiled under the title *Rome Hath Spoken* (Chicago: Franciscan Herald Press, 1932). Maurin may have read these individually and then become aware of this compilation.

38. Maurin, "The Case for Utopia," *Worker*, April 1934, p. 3. By the fall of 1934, at Maurin's direction, Agostino Gemilli's *The Franciscan Message to the World* (trans. Henry Louis Hughes [London: Burns, Oates and Washburne, 1934]) was being read at supper to the *Worker* community. Maurin published a compilation of Gemilli's works entitled "From Fr. Gemilli's 'Franciscan Message': Culled by P. Maurin," *Worker*, December 1934, p. 6.

39. See Stanley Vishnewski, "Days of Action: The Story of The Catholic Worker Movement," Vol. 1, unpublished manuscript, ca. 1966, pp. 55–56, DD-CW, Stanley Vishnewski Papers, Series W-12.3, Box 1.

40. Maurin, "Go-Getters vs. Go-Givers," *Worker*, August 1936, p. 4.

41. Maurin, "The Case for Utopia," *Worker*, April 1, 1934, p. 3. On the explosive quality of Francis's message through the centuries and the radical movements that took Francis as their inspiration, see Norman Cohn, *The Pursuit of the Millennium: Revolutionary Millenarians and Mystical Anarchists of the Middle Ages*, revised and expanded edition (New York: Oxford University Press, 1970), p. 157. On the "bureaucratization of the Franciscan charisma," see Lawrence S. Cunningham, *Saint Francis* (Boston: Twayne, 1976), pp. 114–115.

CHAPTER FOUR

1. Stanley Vishnewski, "Days of Action," vol. 1, ca. 1966, pp. 50–51.

2. Ibid., pp. 55–56.

3. Ibid., p. 76.

4. Ibid., pp. 68–72.

5. "Thank You!" *Worker*, May 1, 1934, p. 4.

6. "The Church and Social Problems," *Orate Fratres*, 9 (April 1934): 277; John Toomey, S.J., "Radicals of the Right," *America* 52 (February 2, 1935): 399.

7. J. G. Brunini, "Catholic Paper vs. Communism," *Commonweal* 19 (November 24, 1933): 97.

8. Ibid., pp. 96–98. Maurin's discussions with communists were unusual in their day and controversial. He was attacked by conservative Catholics and communists alike. For the attack by Catholics see *Brooklyn Tablet*, August 24, 1935, pp. 6, 7. For the attack by communists see *Daily Worker*, August 18, 1934, p. 2.

9. John LaFarge, S. J., "Peter the Agitator Quotes the Prophets of Israel," *America* 55 (August 1, 1936): 395.

10. Maurin, "Feeding the Poor," *Worker*, May 1936, p. 4.

11. LaFarge, "Peter the Agitator," p. 395.

12. But if Maritain left with such an impression of the Worker movement, he also wanted to clarify a discussion he had had with Maurin, and stat-

ed: "I'm of the impression that I didn't make myself quite clear on the subject of the Pluralist State, when I replied to your explanation of it. I want to make it quite clear that such a state with its 'Federation' of diverse juridicial structures, would be not merely a simple collection, but would have a real moral unity of orientation. It would deserve the name of Christian because it would tend in a positive fashion, across these diverse structures, toward an integral Christian ideal. Instead of being polarized by a materialistic conception of the world and of life, like the capitalist and the communist state, it would be polarized through the knowledge of the spiritual dignity of the human person and on the love which is due him" (Maritain to Maurin, November 11, 1934, Maurin Papers, Series W-10, Box 1).

13. Maurin, "Big Shots and Little Shots," *Catholic Mind* 32 (July 8, 1934): 260; "Action: Political or Catholic?," *Catholic Mind* 32 (July 22, 1934): 278. The pamphlets were numerous and published by the Catholic Worker Press beginning in 1934; the one-penny pamphlets were mimeographed and the two-penny pamphlets were printed. See DD-CW, Series W-1, Box 1. Also see "Catholic Worker Moves to New House of Hospitality on Charles Street," *Commonweal* 21 (March 1935): 627.

14. *The Daily Catholic Worker* began on May 1 and apparently ended on May 25. For the announcement of its beginning, see "Mimeograph Machines Urged by P. Maurin for Every Parish," *Worker*, May 1, 1934, p. 6. Copies of the mimeographed sheet can be found in DD-CW, Series W-1, Box 1. For comments on the sheets, see "Mustard Seed," *America* 50 (March 24, 1934): 584.

15. Father J. Stanley Murphy, C.S.B., to Maurin, December 2, 1934, Maurin Papers, Series W-10, Box 2; Francis S. Yeager, C.S.B., to Maurin, December 3, 1934, Maurin Papers, Series W-10, Box 2.

16. Day to Murphy, December 6, 1934, DD-CW, Series W-2, Box 1.

17. Day to Bishop, December 7, 1934, DD-CW, Series W-2, Box 1; Day to Miss Bresetle, December 18, 1934, DD-CW, Series W-2, Box 1.

18. "The Catholic Worker and the Negro," *Worker*, May 1934, p. 4.

19. Maurin, "The Bishop's Message: Quotations and Comments," *Worker*, May 1934, p. 2.

20. "Catholic Worker Opens Harlem Office!," *Daily Catholic Worker*, May 22, 1934, p 1, DD-CW, Series W-1, Box 2; "Through Good Samaritan the Catholic Worker Opens Harlem Office on 7th Ave.," *Worker*, June 1, 1934, pp. 1, 2.

21. Herman Hergenhan, "Municipal Lodging House No 'House of Hospitality,' " *Worker*, May 1, 1934, p. 6; ibid., June 1, 1934, p. 5. For a vivid description of Maurin and Hergenhan's relationship, see Dorothy Day, *The Long Loneliness* (New York: Harper and Row, 1952), pp. 192–199.

22. "Catholic Worker Opens Harlem Office," *Worker*, June 1, 1934, p. 2; John LaFarge, S. J., *Reflections on Growing Old* (New York: Doubleday, 1963), p. 125.

NOTES

23. Unsigned to Paul Daley, September 18, 1934, DD-CW, Series W-2, Box 1; editors to Mary G. MacSweney, October 13, 1934, DD-CW, Series W-2, Box 1.

24. "Harlem Program," *Worker*, October 1934, p. 1. See Julia Porcelli Moran interview with Dean Mowrer, Tivoli, New York, 1970, pp. 8–14, DD-CW, Series W-9, Box 1.

25. Maurin, "The Race Problem," *Worker*, May 1938, p. 8. See also idem, "Let's Be Fair to the Negroes for Christ's Sake," *Worker*, September 1941, pp. 1, 8.

26. Unsigned to Father James McVann, C.S.P., October 16, 1934, DD-CW, Series W-2, Box 1; unsigned to Mrs. Montgomery, though evidence suggests these letters were written by Dorothy Day.

27. Vishnewski, "Days of Action," vol. 1, unpublished manuscript, ca. 1958, Vishnewski Papers, Series W-12.3, Box 1; ibid., ca. 1966, p. 80.

28. H. Hergenhan, "C. W. Sympathizers Protect Quarters in Harlem Riot: Story of Night of Watching Told by Manager of Harlem Branch," *Worker*, April 1935, pp. 1, 6.

29. Vishnewski, "Harlem Tempo," *Worker*, October 1935, p. 5; idem, "Days of Action," vol. 1, ca. 1966, p. 74.

30. Hergenhan, "Harlem Riot," *Worker*, April 1935, p. 1.

31. Nicholas Berdyaev, "The Bourgeois Mind," arranged by Peter Maurin, *Worker*, July–August 1935, pp. 5, 7. Maurin arranged several of Berdyaev's writings that were not published. See Berdyaev, "Christianity and Class-War," and "Machines," Maurin Papers, Series W-10, Box 8. Maurin was influenced by the reading of Berdyaev's works in the early 1930s. Books Maurin read included Berdyaev's *The Bourgeois Mind and Other Essays*, trans. Donald Attwater (London: Sheed and Ward, 1934); *Christianity and Class War*, trans. Donald Attwater (New York: Sheed and Ward, 1934); *Freedom and Spirit*, trans. Oliver Clarke (New York: Scribners, 1935); and *The End of Our Time*, trans. Donald Attwater (London: Sheed and Ward, 1933).

32. Maurin, "In the Light of History," *Worker*, June 1935, pp.1, 8. See also idem, "Five Forms of Capitalism," *Worker*, March 1942, pp. 3, 5.

33. On the evils of secularization, see Maurin, "For Catholic Action," *Worker*, June 1934, pp. 1, 5. For his comments on the Reformation see Maurin, "Beyond Nationalism," *Worker*, June 1941, pp. 1, 2.

34. Maurin, "Easy Essays," *Worker*, May 1933, pp. 1, 8; idem, "Not Jewish Wealth but Irish Culture," *Worker*, December 1940, p. 4; idem, "Is Inflation Inevitable?," *Worker*, December 15, 1933, p. 1; idem, "The Case for Utopia," *Worker*, April 1, 1934, pp. 1, 3.

35. Emmanuel Mounier, *A Personalist Manifesto*, trans. Monks of St. John's Abbey (London: Longmans, Green, 1938), p. 6.

36. Maurin, "Institutions vs. Corporations—Catholic Tactic," *Worker*, December 1935, p. 2; idem, "Communitarian Personalism," *Worker*, September 1936, p. 1.

PETER MAURIN

CHAPTER FIVE

1. Maurin, "Back to Christ!—Back to the Land!," *Worker*, November 1935, pp. 1, 8.

2. Maurin rarely addressed this question of culture in detail but suggested it in a variety of ways (see Maurin, "Outdoor Universities," *Worker*, January 1937, pp. 1, 7, and Arthur Sheehan, "Interview with Peter Maurin," *Worker*, April 1943, p. 7). To Sheehan's question on the interaction of culture, cultivation, and cult, Maurin replied, "If too much attention is paid to one to the detriment of another, things go wrong. There must be a balance. Different persons have different inclinations. Those whose inclination is to work with their hands will become disgruntled if too much time is given to discussion. If not enough time is given to discussion and there is too much physical work, the intellectually minded will fall away." What made for good morale on a farming commune? "It comes from harmony when the emphasis on prayer, discussion, and work is rightly balance'" (see Sheehan, "Interview," *Worker*, April 1943, p. 7).

3. Maurin, "Back to Christ!," *Worker*, November 1935, p. 8.

4. H. Hergenhan, "Farming Commune," *Worker*, June 1935, p. 5.

5. Dorothy Day, *Loaves and Fishes* (New York: Harper and Row, 1953), p. 43.

6. Ibid., p. 44.

7. Maurin would gather in the garden those who came to see him and hoe in hand would start teaching: "Bishop von Ketteler says that we are bound under pain of mortal sin to relieve the extreme needs of our poorer brother with our superfluous goods. But with our superfluous goods we build white elephants like the Empire State Building. With our superfluous goods we build power houses which increase producing power and therefore increase unemployment." Day commented that each of those statements was good for a day of discussion about charity, personal and state responsibility, village industries and decentralization (see Day, *Loaves and Fishes*, pp. 44–45).

8. Cyril Echele, "An Idea of a Farming Commune," *Worker*, February 1936, pp. 2, 6.

9. "Farming Commune 70 Miles Distant Marks Beginning," *Worker*, April 1936, pp. 1, 6.

10. "More about the Farming Commune," *Worker*, April 1936, p. 8.

11. Dorothy Weston Coddington, "Cult, Culture, and Cultivation," *Liturgy and Sociology* 1 (Summer 1936): 15.

12. Maurin, *Easy Essays* (New York: Sheed and Ward, 1936).

13. Dorothy Day, "Peter's Book Here at Last," *Worker*, July 1936, pp. 1, 2.

14. Day to Deverall, September 24, 1935, DD-CW, Series W-2, Box 1; Deverall to Day, September 20, 21, 25, 1935, DD-CW, Series W-2.2, Box 1.

15. Day, *The Long Loneliness* (New York: Harper and Row, 1952), p. 180.

16. Arthur G. Falls, "The Chicago Letter," *Worker*, June 1936, p. 3; Monsignor John Hays' interview with Francis Joseph Sicius, June 1976, Chicago, Illinois, quoted in Francis Joseph Sicius, "The Chicago Catholic Worker

Movement, 1936 to the Present," (Ph.D. diss., Loyola University of Chicago, 1979), p. 57.

17. Falls, "Chicago Letter," *Worker*, August 1936, p. 3.

18. "Boston Crowd Opens Workers' Hospice and Food Center," *Worker*, May 1936, p. 2.

19. Echele to the editors, *Worker*, November 1936, p. 2.

20. "Houses of Hospitality," *Worker*, December 1936, p. 4; Barbara Wall to Day, September 25, 1935, DD-CW, Series W-4, Box 7.

21. Maurin continued: "Catholic teachers/ teaching in Catholic or public schools/ who do not know how to present/ Catholic social thought,/ either to men on the street/ or to the pupils in the schools,/ will be interested to learn/ that a Protestant agitator/ well known in Union Square/ is presenting the Thomistic doctrine/ of the common good/ to the men of the street/ in the streets of Harlem" (Maurin, "Communist Action in Schools Challenge to Catholics, Declares Peter Maurin," *Worker*, July–August 1934, p. 3).

22. Maurin, "The Pluralist State," *Worker*, November 1936, pp. 1, 6. Maurin's understanding that the power of the state should be minimized and ideally eliminated was controversial to those outside the movement. To many it seemed anarchistic, even conservative. But the state was only chaotic or protective of vested interests in a society pursuing affluence. In a functional society comprised of villages and subsistence homesteads, the energy that the modern state provided was useless, perhaps even destructive. Like bureaucracy, the state assumed responsibilities best left to the person; the assumption of these responsibilities by the state deprived the person of his integrity and rendered him passive.

23. Barry to the Editors, *Worker*, February 1937, p. 5.

24. Degnan to Barry, *Worker*, February 1937, p. 5.

25. Maurin, "Back to Newmanism," *Worker*, December 1936, p. 3.

26. Ibid.

27. Maurin, "Outdoor Universities," *Worker*, January 1937, pp. 1, 7.

28. Arthur Sheehan, "Peter and Harvard," *The Candle*, mimeograph sheet, ca. 1949, pp. 1, 3, Sheehan Papers, Series W-15, Box 1; Sheehan, *Peter Maurin: Gay Believer* (New York: Hanover House, 1959), pp. 166–167. Maurin's agitation for houses of hospitality near secular universities came to fruition in March 1940 at Yale University. See Harold Sullivan to Day, March 28, 1940, DD-CW, Series W-4, Box 2; and Sullivan to the Editor, *Worker*, May 1940, p. 7.

29. Maurin, "The Thinking Journalist," *Worker*, February 1937, pp. 1, 3.

30. Maurin, "Social Workers and Workers," in Peter Maurin, *Catholic Radicalism: Phrased Essays for the Green Revolution* (New York: Catholic Worker Books, 1949), p. 74.

31. Day, "C. W. States Stand on Strikes," *Worker*, July 1936, pp. 1, 2.

32. "A Philosophy of Work by Eric Gill," arranged by Peter Maurin, *Worker*, January 1941, p. 6. Maurin arranged many of Gill's works on the subject of industrialization and labor and published them in the *Worker*. See "Men and Machinery," *Worker*, June 1934; "Politics of Industrialism," *Work-*

er, September 1934; "Unemployment," *Worker*, October 1945. See also Maurin's unpublished arrangement of Gill's work "Work and Culture," and "Christianity and the Machine Age," Maurin Papers, Series W-10, Box 4.

33. Day, *The Long Loneliness*, pp. 220, 221.

34. "New Association for Catholics in Labor Movement," *Worker*, March 1937, p. 1. For information on ACTU, see Neil Betten, *Catholic Activism and the Industrial Worker* (Gainesville: University of Florida, 1976), pp. 124–145.

35. John C. Cort, "Dorothy Day at 75," *Commonweal* 98 (February 23, 1973): 476.

36. Maurin, "The Sit-Down Technique," *Worker*, April 1937, pp. 1, 6.

37. Maurin, "Peter Maurin Explains," *Worker*, November 1937, p. 4. The previous discussion, ibid., pp. 1, 4.

38. William R. O'Connor, "Primitive Christianity in New York City," *The Ecclesiastical Review* 96 (March 1937): 231, 233.

CHAPTER SIX

1. "Monthly Symposium on Personalist Democracy," January 1938, p. 1, DD-CW, Series W-10, Box 1.

2. Roger N. Baldwin, "Remarks on the Philosophy of Personalism," in "Monthly Symposium," p. 1.

3. Eugene Kohn, "Religious Principles in Social Reconstruction," in "Monthly Symposium," p. 2.

4. Ibid., p. 3.

5. Rev. A. J. Muste, "Remarks on Personalist Democracy," in "Monthly Symposium," p. 3.

6. Maurin, "Personalist Essays," in "Monthly Symposium," pp. 5, 6. Maurin was involved in at least three more symposia but only one other transcript of the meetings apparently survives. See the digest of the March 1938 session in DD-CW, Series W-10, Box 1.

7. Jacques Maritain, "Twilight of Civilization," arranged by Peter Maurin, *Worker*, January 1940, p. 3; Don Luigi Sturzo, "Spirit of Democracy," arranged by Peter Maurin, *Worker*, March 1940, p. 8. Maurin read two of Sturzo's books, *Politics and Morality*, trans. Barbara Barclay Carter (London: Burns, Oates and Washbourne, 1938), and *Church and State*, trans. Barbara Barclay Carter (London: G. Bles, 1939).

8. Maurin, "Personalist Democracy," *Worker*, November 1939, pp. 1, 3.

9. "May Day—Mary's Day," *Worker*, May 1938, p. 4.

10. Brother Matthew, "Bishop on Land," *Worker*, May 1938, pp. 5, 8.

11. "Farming Commune," *Worker*, June 1938, p. 4.

12. Day, "Idea for a Farm Commune," *Worker*, January 1938, p. 8.

13. Ibid.

14. Alfred Grosch, "Why Not a Peasantry?," arranged by Peter Maurin, *Worker*, January 1937, p. 8.

15. Vrest Orton, "A Village Experiment," arranged by Peter Maurin, *Worker*, September 1937, p. 4.

NOTES

16. Vishnewski, "Days of Action," unpublished manuscript, vol. 2, ca. 1966, p. 298, Vishnewski Papers, Series 12.3, Box 1.

17. Dominican Sisters of Grand Rapids, "Cult, Holy Mass," arranged by Peter Maurin, Maurin Papers, Series W-10, Box 3; Christopher Dawson, "Culture Rooted in Religion," arranged by Peter Maurin, Maurin Papers, Series W-10, Box 3; Herbert Agar, "Cultivation," arranged by Peter Maurin, Maurin Papers, Series W-10, Box 3. Maurin published one arrangement of Dawson's work: see "Catholicism and the Bourgeois Mind," *Worker*, January 1936. Maurin was an avid reader of Dawson's works. Among others, Maurin read Dawson's *Progress and Religion: An Historical Inquiry* (New York: Longmans, Green, 1929); *Christianity and the New Age* (London: Sheed and Ward, 1931); *Enquiries into Religion and Culture* (New York: Sheed and Ward, 1933). In reference to Herbert Agar, Maurin read Agar's *Land of the Free* (Boston: Houghton Mifflin, 1935), and *Who Owns America?* (Boston: Houghton Mifflin, 1936).

18. Vishnewski, "Days of Action," vol. 2., ca. 1966, p. 297.

19. Day, "Peter Maurin," unpublished manuscript, ca. 1948, p. 145, DD-CW, Series D-3, Box 2.

20. Vishnewski, "Days of Action," vol. 2, ca. 1966, p. 299.

21. Maurin to Day, December 28, 1938; January 19, 1939; February 19, 1939; Maurin Papers, Series W-10, Box 2.

22. Cassidy to C.W., March 10, 1939, DD-CW, Series W-2.2, Box 1.

23. Cassidy to Day, March 20, 1939, DD-CW, Series W-2.2, Box 1.

24. Cassidy, "Peter Maurin," under the pseudonym Mary Macard, March 1, 1939, DD-CW, Series W-2.2, Box 1.

25. William Gauchat, "Log," unpublished diaries, vol. 3, May 30, 1939, p. 25, Our Lady of the Wayside Home, Avon, Ohio.

26. Gauchat, "Log," vol. 5, March 1, 1940, p. 78.

27. Ibid., pp. 78, 79.

28. Sheehan, *Candle*, mimeograph, ca. 1947, unpaged, Sheehan Papers, Series W-15, Box 3. Sheehan came to the Worker and worked closely with Maurin, eventually becoming editor of the paper for a year. However, his wholehearted response to Maurin's message, including poverty and agitation, was not without its family complications (See Elizabeth Sheehan to the author, September 25, 1979, personal correspondence).

29. Arthur Sheehan, "Conversations with Peter," in *Peter Maurin: Christian Radical: Essays and Reminiscences of the Founder of The Catholic Worker Movement* (St. Louis: Pio Decimo Press, 1950), p. 11.

30. Ibid.

31. Day, "Open Letter to Peter Maurin From Editor," *Worker*, June 1939, p. 1.

32. Ibid.

33. Ibid., p. 4. Maurin was evidently serious about not coming back, at least for a time, and considered opening a place in Dallas that would combine his teaching French with the offering of some form of hospitality (see Elizabeth Burrow to Dorothy Day, May 5, 1939, factual excerpt from Dorothy

Day's restricted personal correspondence provided by the Marquette Archives). This was not the only time Maurin had threatened to leave nor would it be the last. See Day, *The Long Loneliness*, (New York: Harper and Row, 1952), pp. 180, 181.

34. Vishnewski, "Peter Maurin to Lead Classes at Easton Farm," June 1940, p. 8.

35. Erwin Mooney, "Peter Maurin Begins Summer School," *Worker*, July–August 1940, p. 3.

36. Martin Paul interview with Deane Mowrer, n.d., Tivoli, New York, DD-CW, Series W-9, Box 1, pp. 9–12. On his travels Maurin wrote regularly to Dorothy Day. See his letters to Day on October 23, November 9, and November 27, 1939, Maurin Papers, Series W-10, Box 2.

37. Mignon Virginia McMenamy, "A Man of Charity," quoted in Sheehan, *Peter Maurin: Christian Radical*, p. 17.

38. Ibid., p. 18.

CHAPTER SEVEN

1. Maurin, "Utilitarians, Futilitarians, Totalitarians," *Worker*, June 1937, p. 1.

2. Maurin, "Caesarism or Personalism" *Worker*, March 1937, pp. 1, 2.

3. For a discussion of these issues see "Here We Go Again," *Worker*, January 1938, p. 1; "Machinery Is All Ready for Next War," *Worker*, July–August 1939, p. 3; "Fight Conscription," *Worker*, September 1939, p. 1; "To the Workers: An Appeal to Workers to Sacrifice for Peace," *Worker*, October 1939, pp. 1, 3.

4. Dorothy Day, "Thoughts on Breadlines and on the War," *Worker*, June 1940, pp. 1, 4. See also William D. Miller, *A Harsh and Dreadful Love: Dorothy Day and the Catholic Worker Movement* (New York: Liveright, 1973), pp. 154–170.

5. Day to Fellow Worker, August 10, 1940, DD-CW, Series W-6.3, Box 1.

6. Maurin, "War and Peace," *Worker*, December 1937, pp. 1, 8. Also *Daily Catholic Worker*, n.d., no. 6, DD-CW, Series W-1, Box 1.

7. Maurin, "Peace Preparedness," *Worker*, April 1938, p. 1.

8. Ibid.

9. Cardinal Innitzer, "Peace and War," arranged by Peter Maurin, *Worker*, September 1939, p. 3.

10. Eric Gill, "Work and War," arranged by Peter Maurin, *Worker*, December 1939, p. 6.

11. Arthur Sheehan, *Peter Maurin: Gay Believer* (New York: Hanover House, 1959), p. 199; Heaney to Father Kenpenny, January 2, [1942?], Nina Polcyn Moore Papers, Series W-17, Box 1; Dorothy Day, *The Long Loneliness* (New York: Harper and Row, 1952), pp. 180, 181.

12. See Maurin, "Easy Essays," *Worker*, May 1933, p. 8; Maurin, "Interview with Moley Told by Peter Maurin," *Worker*, December 15, 1933, p. 7;

NOTES

"Monthly Symposium on Personalist Democracy," January 1938, DD-CW, Series W-10, Box 1.

13. Maurin, "Let's Keep the Jews for Christ's Sake," *Worker*, July–August 1939, p. 1.

14. Maurin, "Why Pick on the Jews?" *Worker*, January 1940, pp. 1, 2.

15. Leon Bloy, "Salvation Is of the Jews," arranged by Peter Maurin, *Worker*, July–August 1942, p. 2.

16. Ibid., pp. 1, 2. Also see Maurin's unpublished manuscripts, "Jews in New York," Maurin Papers, Series W-10, Box 3 and Father Dieux, "For Israel," arranged by Peter Maurin, Maurin Papers, Series W-10, Box 3.

17. Maurin, "A New Venture," *Worker*, January 1940, p. 2. For the beginning of the center see Vishnewski, "Days of Action," vol. 2, ca. 1958, p. 330, Vishnewski Papers, Series 12.3, Box 1; and Joe Zarrella to Dorothy Day, December 29, 1939. This is an excerpt from Dorothy Day's restricted personal correspondence provided by the Marquette Archives.

18. Maurin, "Judaism and Catholicism," *Worker*, February 1940, p. 2. The emphasis that Maurin placed on the conversion of Jews is substantiated in his essays and in the following sources. In his unpublished manuscript, vol. 2, ca. 1958, Vishnewski stated, "Peter is interested in opening a store to run for the conversion of the Jewish people.... Father Krimm, a Redemptorist, is interested in the project and has promised to act as a spiritual advisor to any prospective Jewish converts" (330). When interviewed by the author on the subject of Maurin and the Jews, Vishnewski replied, "I think he would have loved to have seen them become converted, because he felt that the Christ was the Messiah, and that if the Jews became Catholics, they became 100% Jews. That's what he believed in" (20). See Vishnewski interview with the author, New York City, May 1978, p. 20, DD-CW, Series W-9, Box 2. In *The Candle*, Arthur Sheehan wrote: "It was in Boston....that Peter made me deeply aware of the importance of this apostolate. He had an Elias-like desire to bring the Jews to the faith, but he was well aware of the difficulties. He would talk for days about them—their many divisions of thought, their restless craving for a philosophy to live by, their Messianism. If they had largely abandoned the idea of a personal Messiah it was only to take up the idea of a Messianic people—one destined to lead the world in all the arts and sciences. When they pointed to Einstein, Menuhin and the endless line of Jewish greats, it was simple to see how the idea endured. The Zionist dream of a state was just a small cloud on the horizon" (Sheehan, "Peter and the Jews," *The Candle*, ca. 1949, unpaged, Sheehan Papers, Series W-15, Box 3). See also Sheehan, *Maurin*, pp. 194, 195. Both Vishnewski and Sheehan were participants in the center.

19. "Invitation," *Worker*, September 1940, p. 4.

20. Sheehan, *Maurin*, p. 194.

21. Goldstein to Sheehan, November 26, 1940, DD-CW, Series W-2.1, Box 3.

22. Ibid. With reference to Goldstein, Sheehan writes, "[Maurin] offered

to pass the place over to David Goldstein, noted Jewish convert and writer from Boston. Goldstein refused to come to New York without a formal invitation from diocesan authorities." However, Goldstein recommended his book, *Jewish Panorama* (Boston: Catholic Campaigners for Christ, 1940) and his pamphlet, "The Call to Israel" as help. See Sheehan, *Peter Maurin: Gay Believer*, p. 194.

23. Joe Zarrella to Dorothy Day, ca. 1940. Factual excerpt from Dorothy Day's restricted personal correspondence provided by the Marquette Archives. For Sheehan's reflection on the Jews, see Sheehan, "Purim," *Worker*, September 1943, p. 2; Sheehan, "Peter and the Jews," *The Candle*; Sheehan tape, Sheehan Papers, Series W-9.1, File C-9.

24. "Round Table Discussions," *Worker*, December 1940, p. 3.

25. "Farm School," *Worker*, June 1941, p. 6; Dorothy Gauchat interview with the author, Avon, Ohio, May 23, 1978, pp. 4–8, DD-CW, Series W-9, Box 1. See also Sheehan, "Interview with Peter Maurin," *Worker*, May 1943, p. 3; Sheehan, "Interview," *Worker*, June 1943, p. 12.

26. Maurin, "The Pope and the World," *Worker*, December 1941, p. 6.

27. Eric Gill, "On Poverty," arranged by Peter Maurin, *Worker*, December 1941, p. 7.

28. "Alcuin Community: A School of Social Reconstruction," pamphlet, ca. 1940, DD-CW, Series W-4, Box 7; David Mason, "Hegira with Peter," *Worker*, September 1943, p. 8; McMenamy, "A Man of Charity," in *Peter Maurin: Christian Radical: Essays and Reminiscences of the Founder of the Catholic Worker Movement* (St. Louis: Pio Decimo Press, 1950), p. 16.

29. Mason, "Hegira With Peter," *Worker*, September 1943, p. 8.

30. Day, "Day After Day," *Worker*, September 1943, p. 8.

31. Maurin, et al., "We Carry On," *Worker*, October 1943, p. 2

32. Day, "Farming Commune," *Worker*, February 1944, pp. 1, 8.

33. Ibid., p 8; "The Catholic Worker Retreat House," *Worker*, October 1944, p. 2.

34. Day, "Peter Maurin," unpublished manuscript, ca. 1948, pp. 152–153, DD-CW, Series D-3, Box 2.

35. Vishnewski, "Days of Action," vol. 2, ca. 1966, pp. 413, 417, Vishnewski Papers, Series W-12.3, Box 1; Sheehan, *Peter Maurin: Gay Believer*, p. 201. The compilations of Gill's works that Maurin arranged were published over the next few years: see Gill's "This Is Matriarchy," *Worker*, January 1945; "Unemployment," *Worker*, October 1945; "Where Are We Going?" *Worker*, November 1947.

36. Day, "On Pilgrimage," *Worker*, June 1946, p. 2; Day, "On Pilgrimage," *Worker*, July–August 1946, p. 7.

37. Day, "On Pilgrimage," *Worker*, April 1947, p. 3.

38. "The Story of Three Deaths," *Worker*, June 1949, p. 2.

39. "Mott Street," *Worker*, March 1948, p. 2.

40. Day, "Without Poverty We Are Powerless," *Worker*, May 1948, p. 2.

41. Ibid.

42. Day, "The Story of Three Deaths," *Worker*, June 1949, p. 2.

NOTES

CHAPTER EIGHT

1. "Poor Man," *Time*, May 30, 1949, p. 54; "La Morte di Peter Maurin, Apostolo Dei Lavoratori," *L'Osservatore Romano*, July 6, 1949, p 6; "Peter Maurin, 71, Catholic Leader: Founder of Worker Movement is Dead—Formed Hospitality Houses to Shelter Needy," *New York Times*, May 17, 1949, p. 25.

2. Richter to Dorothy Day, May 18, 1949, Maurin Papers, Series W-10, Box 1; Moody to Day, May 21, 1949, Maurin Papers, Series W-10, Box 1; Gunn, "In appreciative memory of my friend and teacher Peter Maurin," May 17, 1949, Maurin Papers, Series W-10, Box 1.

3. John McKeon, "Poverty's Progress: Lament for a Chief," *Worker*, June 1949, p. 3.

4. Cogley's involvement with the Worker movement is documented in Francis Joseph Sicius, "The Chicago Catholic Worker Movement, 1936 to Present" (Ph.D. diss. Loyola University of Chicago, 1979). Merton carried on an extensive (and restricted) correspondence with Dorothy Day while publishing numerous articles in the *Worker* from April 1949 to June 1968; see James A. Forest, "Thomas Merton and the Catholic Worker: Ten Years After," *Worker*, December 1978, pp. 4, 5. Daniel Berrigan continually refers to the Worker movement as the hope of the future. See his article on Maurin, "They Say I Am Crazy Because I Refuse to Be Crazy the Way Everybody Else Is Crazy," *Worker*, May 1977, pp. 1, 5, 11.

5. See Henry J. Nouwen, *The Wounded Healer: Ministry in Contemporary Society* (New York: Doubleday, 1972); and Ernst Friedrich Schumacher, *Small Is Beautiful: Economics as if People Mattered* (New York: Harper and Row, 1973). The movement back to the land has continued among people affiliated with the Worker movement. For the latest endeavor see Peggy Scherer, "Peter Maurin Farm," *Worker*, October–November 1979, p. 1.

6. Paul Hanly Furfey, "Unemployment on the Land," *Worker*, October 1939, p. 8; idem, "There Are Two Kinds of Agrarians," *Worker*, December 1939, pp. 1, 8; John Cort, "Reform Begins at the Plant Level," *Commonweal* 48 (October 1, 1948): 597; idem, "Is a Christian Industrialism Possible?," *Commonweal* 49 (October 29, 1948): 60–62; idem, "Christian Industrialism III," *Commonweal* 49 (November 26, 1948): 174, 175. The questions of agrarianism, industrialism, population, and religiosity are complex and difficult to answer. Answers to these questions depend heavily on one's orientation toward, and perception of, the social and religious order. As we have suggested in the Introduction, Maurin looked at reality through the eyes of a prophet. Thus, though he would defend the practicality of his thoughts, in the final analysis they were based on his understanding of salvation. In Maurin's eyes, once the basis of salvation was established there was no turning back; life had to be oriented around it.

7. Aldous Huxley, *Brave New World* (London: Chatto and Windus, 1932); George Orwell, *Animal Farm* (New York: Harcourt, Brace, 1946): idem, *1984* (New York: Harcourt, Brace, 1949).

8. Maurin, "For a New Order," *Worker*, April 1942, p. 7.